Atlantic City

Dice Lies Video Tape

DICE LIES

VIDEO TAPE

A Novel by: Stevie G

Edited by: Ernest L. McDuffie, Ph.D.

Stephanie,

Enjoy, thanks for
your support.

Introduction:

This is a city where in the mid 1980's, something new was always right around the corner but there's a price for everything. You must be true, believe in yourself, just be you, there's nothing more unique than you as a person or human. Respect is earn not given, it's a two-way street. Never allow anyone to make you feel less, some people will like you, some won't. Every day you get a new opportunity to learn something new as Atlantic City goes through its newest transformation, the casino's, this city is one big stage. You must be careful of the part that you play, it's very easy to fall for anything if you don't stand for something! It's important to know when to be your own beacon of hope because you can lose yourself very easy in Atlantic City.

Table of Content:

<u>Before the Incident, Life was Good!</u>

This is how the story went.

IN 1985 THE CITY WAS AT ITS peak. It was all about money, preferably cash. No one was expecting this type of money to come into Atlantic City, and if they didn't come to Atlantic City on their own, we went and picked them up from different states or countries. We called them junkets, if you had enough people to fill up an airplane, we would provide the airplane. If you have enough people to fill up a bus, we will provide the bus. All we asked was to show us that you had some money or collateral like a business, a house, a building, a baseball team, a basketball team, or a football team. Who cares where you got the money from, you just couldn't go over $9,999.99 in cash without involving paperwork? This made my job was simple. Dice was my game, I didn't want any other games I just had to be the best at, I didn't need anything else, just dice. My crew, I used to roll with was the Steubenville Ohio Boys, ninety percent of them were Italian, but they made sure that the rest of the crew was very versatile. We had farmers, teachers, every kind of ethnic background and color you could think of, but it seemed like everyone was learning from the Italians. Some things became habit-forming, you could find yourself saying Italian phrases easy. John Sasini and the Rotundo brothers, it was all about fashion, and the exclamation mark was the knot in your tie.

The Florio brothers, I really admired them, Tommy and Jerry, their uncle was the governor of New Jersey Tom Florio, that didn't hurt. They took dressing and fashion to a whole other level, from the suits to the shirts, shoes, and most of all ties. Once I became a manager on the craps table, it was time to step up my game.

I couldn't pick a better role model to show me how to dress or talk to clients and walk the walk and talk the talk better than Tommy D, he was the man. He was the dude straight out of *GQ* magazine, but he was always cracking jokes, I recall asking Tommy,

"How do I make a knot that small in a tie like that?"

"Do you know how you normally tie your ties?"

"Yeah!"

"Well, the next time you make a knot in your tie, put your foot against the bathroom sink and pull that shit until it's a small knot or until you turn blue in the face and pass the fuck out." I called him a smart ass because he was a jokester on the casino floor.

"But the only true way to achieve that look is to go to Eleganza Menswear."

"They're on Atlantic Avenue across from the old Pep Boys in Atlantic City, right?"

"No, that's where they used to be, now they're in the casino, but they're moving to the Ocean Club soon. Ask for Larry, Gino or the old man, tell him Tommy D sent you to buy a tie, so you can start your tie collection." So, I did. My father used to always say, "I want you to learn how to tie a tie just like Kojak or Ronald Reagan." I just couldn't tell my wife how much I paid for the ties, or suits, he even had a lay-away plan just for me and at that time, I became one of the biggest Giorgio Armani and Versace fans in the city. Gino would sell me the winter suits in the spring, the spring suits, he would sell them to me in the fall with a small Vig on them.

The main thing that the casino crew strove for was to keep our clients here at our joint. We made the clients feel that when they came down to our joint in Atlantic City, they know they're going to have a great time and be treated like a king.

All my clients were different, some were lawyers, some were doctors, some have businesses, some own franchises, baseball teams, football teams, we didn't discriminate. We would fly you in from wherever you wanted to come from and fly your ass back home. You knew when you left our casino you were completely satisfied, and you enjoyed yourself fully. That's how we built our reputation.

A lot of it started with the Steve Wynn organization, he set new standards and expectations. I had a little brown book with all my high rollers' personal information including phone numbers.

I could tell you what my players drink, how many drinks it takes to get them drunk, the names of the restaurants they like, clubs they enjoy, who was the wife and who was the side piece without the embarrassment, what their average bets and buy-ins were. My main objective was to keep my clients at the crap table for as long as possible. We could talk about anything you want it didn't matter. Some of my clients would ask the casino managers when I was working, or I was requested by a player to handle their table.

Most of the time they had to convince us they were broke and hungry to feed them. We had real loan sharks on the casino floor daily who would not hesitate to give a player a loan with 45 to 65 percent interest rates.

Atlantic City had more little gangsters than big mobsters, most of the big mob bosses out of New York, New Jersey and Philadelphia were on a ban list from the casinos. If they did come in, they kept it moving, most of my clients came to play, not to stay.

They could pull out a lump of cash, $40,000 to $140,000 or more, at any given moment. You could hear someone callout, "$26,000 across buy the 4 and 10." and 7 out the next roll, we had real gamblers with real gangster money.

I had one high roller who was real racist. I dealt with

him because he didn't hide it, we used to call him Alabama. He was about 4'4" and weighed about 350 pounds. He would look for me even when I was just a dealer because my crap games always sounded real, like you were playing cello or street dice, he loved me on the stick calling the dice. Always a perfect gentleman until he's had five drinks in him, he then became the KKK. Alabama would get right next to me when I was on stick and whispers, "Boy, what's my point? The gun is loaded, and I got the sheet in the car!" If the dice landed on 11, I would whisper back to him, "Yo lev yo lev, yo momma!" He would come back again with, "Boy, what's my point? The gun is loaded, and I got the sheet in the car!" My next call would be, "Outttt 7."

I had no problem with taking his money, once I became a manager he would still look for me because he knew that I knew, that he didn't mean any harm on the table besides, he would be the first one to tell you that he's a piece of shit and burp in your face, sometimes we had to wheel his fat ass up to a room just to let him sober up a little, you had to have tough skin in this industry.

Another high roller I recall starting my shift at ten in the morning when the casinos would open back up for the day. My client bought in for $80,000 in cash and got a marker for a hundred thousand dollars more, he always made it obvious that he came to play, not to stay.

By one-thirty in the afternoon, my table was up, and I had him stuck for $580,000. We were having fun. What a great afternoon. However, at 5:30 p.m. he had my crap table stuck for $1,150,000. Hey, let the chips fall where they may. He gave it all back that night except for $250,000. As long as he gives the house a chance to win back their money, we're good, the rush is only temporary. The key is to make them feel comfortable enough to stay at that table and gamble.

After a lot of the big action always meeting new people, I made it a point to make my reputation known to interested high rollers. We can talk about anything you want to or just gamble. Ninety-nine-point nine percent of the time my table would go up in limits just because of the action on my game, dealers were happy to work on my games. It seemed like it was one big party my game was always loaded with action that's how the day would move right along. Always the main objective of the table games manager is to watch the money, then watch the bank and most of all, watch your dice.

As a manager they teach you to trust no one, because everyone has an angel and most of all, protect our money. Which was cool, I'll watch your money and count your money, but I'm not going to fight or die for your money! That's what you have security for.

I recall watching a little old man take the dice and hold them in the air as he shook them, he stopped with his hand in the air and looked to the left of him toward his friend and said that he felt faint, he fell straight back on the floor with the dice in his hand. Although I did summon for help, I had to keep my eyes on his hand with my dice in them.

So, I told my box man to watch the bank I had to keep my eyes on my dice no matter what, not to mention the dealer's, even your friends will set you up. Trust them as far as you can throw their ass. When it comes down to your job and money, *trust no one*! Finally, security showed up.

Once they gave me back my dice, everyone was afraid to touch these dice, the table got quiet, the dice were cold, the man was cold, the players called them killer dice. We replaced them with new ones, and that quick, the table got hot again. You never know what someone else's issues are until that moment.

As a matter of fact, I had a good friend, well I thought he was a good friend, until he tried to pass chips on my game when I used to sit box on the crap table. This man I knew for years, I've even lent him money before, he had real fast hands, but fortunately, I was good at my job and my game. Knowing how to use the mirrors on the crap table, I could look in one direction while talking to someone and see everything that was going on behind me through my mirrors. It is a very effective technique.

It would only take me a second to validate the roll of the dice then shift my eyes to the mirror and see what the dealer was doing. This dumb ass was taking green chips off his stack out of the house money and saying check change, as if the man who was next to him had given the chips to him. Well, I saw the man who walked up next to the dealer and his dirty ass didn't have any $25 green chips in his rail. They were all red $5 chips, not to mention I saw him make a stupid ass move with his hands and the bank stack. I shook my head to make sure I was seeing what I thought, and a few minutes later he did it again. "Check change $100" the dealer called out. Because I was focused on him, I saw the whole move in slow motion this time. I couldn't believe this guy and was deeply hurt! I knew his family, but he put me in a bad position, what if management already knew he was a piece of shit?

When he went on a break to the dealers' lounge, I confronted him and called him into the locker room. I pushed him against the locker and asked him, "What the fuck is wrong with you?"

"What do you mean?"

"You know what I mean, that piece of shit that you're passing chips to."

"What? Come on man, you didn't see me do anything."

"I'll tell you what, only you and I know what I saw and if you do it again, you'll get what you deserve it's your call."

"I don't know what you're talking about!"

"Okay!"

I was glad the day was ending, but I had to figure this shit out. *What happens if he's on my game tomorrow?* I had to ask myself. *Where's my loyalty at, with this piece of shit or my bread and butter for my family?* That night on the way home I saw my juice, C-Note. Juice is when someone higher than you in management has your back if you get in trouble. I told him what I thought I saw. Hoping I was wrong but still covering myself since now I'm not the only person who knows something fishy may have happened on that game.

Maybe I was wrong, maybe not. If he never did it again, he'll be fine. Time would tell. The next day when I checked my schedule, I noticed I was on a different table two games down from the previous one. If I really wasn't imagining things, this so-called friend really wasn't a friend and could care less about me or my family.

One hour before the shift was over, the DGE (Division of Gaming Enforcement)/NJ State Police walked up to the game that this fool was on. They asked him to set the dice stick down, put his hands behind his back and they handcuffed him. As he walked away, he wouldn't make eye contact with me. The box man who was on the game and said he saw everything, got suspended for not doing shit. PYA, *Protect Your Ass,* always is the best policy.

It was very simple, either you were good at what you did, or you had juice. Juice could be a good thing or a bad thing, your juice can be there one day and gone the next day but when you have both, skills and juice, the sky's the limit.

Managers will go beyond the limit to get you to be on their team, there was talk about Barron Hilton coming to Atlantic City. Everyone wanted to be a part of that, it was very exciting. So, the crew started putting a team together; Bucky Howard, the Rotundo brothers, John Sicini (a.k.a. C-Note), Big Dominic, George (a.k.a. Mr. Wilson), and lots more.

The Hilton was going to be a guaranteed moneymaker. Everyone began to leave their old jobs and went over there to get the Hilton ready. One of the top executives from the Hilton could not obtain a casino license for some reason from the NJ Casino Control Commission, (CCC). Because of that the Hilton went up for sale and was purchased by Donald Trump and renamed Trump Castle. The very same people I turned down at Trump Plaza because I didn't want any part of Trump's organization and its bullshit, we're now running the Trump Castle Hotel and Casino. Nobody in their right mind wanted to be stuck with Trump!

But for me it was all about my crew, I made sure that you knew of me. Even old man Dave, the bathroom attendee would always say to me,

"Cutty Cutty my main buddy." as he would check my tie in the morning to make sure it had that (Bamm) on it.

My crew was strong, I recall getting comp to go see this great fabulous opera tenor sing at Resorts, Luciano Pavarotti. After the show, there was a line to take pictures with him, it seemed that I was the only black man in that line. I was cool wearing all cafe-skin leather from Jules menswear from AC. The security guard who was handling the line knew me. He moved me to the front of the line, when it was my turn to have my picture with Mr. Pavarotti, I greeted him in an Italian slang saying "Wussup!"

"You speak Italian?"

"Capeesh!" He burst out laughing and started speaking in Italian to me. I burst out laughing as well and told his interpreter, "I was joking, and I don't speak Italian at all, well, maybe just a few words." He burst out laughing as he translated what I was saying to Mr. Pavarotti. He looked at me and burst out laughing, pulling me toward him and giving me a big hug, and told his translator to take a picture of me with him on his personal camera for him, and we all kept laughing. I asked him to autograph the picture and make it out to me and my friend Bob James, who was one of the VIPs at Tropicana Hotel Casino. He did, I thanked him and said my goodbye in my best Italian accent. As I was on my way, Mr. Pavarotti threw up the Black power fist.

I couldn't stop laughing, my Italian wasn't that bad, although it was something that I heard around the crap table all the time. Most of it was just slang. Not understanding one word of any of his songs, but it was very cool to be comp in VIP. Any show that came to town, Patti LaBelle, Luther Vandross, Stephanie Mills, and all the fights, I made it a point to get my VIP comps from my connections. That's what was making Atlantic City the shit, take care of the people and they will keep coming back and send their friends.

When Mike Tyson would come into town for a fight, I would make a point to go downstairs across from the Trump Castle bus depot where they set up a small rink for him to spare. Every break I would go downstairs to see Mike spare until I finally got the chance to talk to him. When I finally did it went something like this, I called out to him, "Brownsville, never ran, never will!" I knew that would get his attention. He turned around and started laughing. "I didn't expect that to come out of a guy who's wearing a suit like that."

I replied, "If the heavyweight champion can come from

Brownsville, a man from Bed-Stuy can wear Armani."

We both started laughing, I was proud of him for just representing Brooklyn and being the champ. Although Bed-Stuy wasn't that far from Brownsville, we still respected each other's hoods. Mike was more impressed by my style of dressing, we laughed and joked about Brooklyn for a minute. As always, I invited him to my crap table and told him if I could do anything for him, that's where I'd be.

The Punch heard around the Castle!

After over a year or more for some strange reason, Mrs. Trump was now running things at the Castle. From the rumors, she made a dollar a week and all the clothes she could buy or some crazy shit.

On June Friday 13, 1986, I was at Viva Lounge at Trump Castle with a few fellows from the crap pit, for one of my bachelors' parties, because tomorrow was my wedding day. The waitress was cool with us. She knew it was my bachelors' party. She brought a round of drinks over to the table and said that they're from the boss over there. As I got up to look and see who it was, to my surprise it was Ivana Trump, I had to go say thank you to her. I straightened up my tie as I walked over to thank Mrs. Trump for the drinks. She said congratulations on my wedding day and wished me the best of luck.

When I returned to work after the honeymoon, the new joke around the Castle was Ivana was the only female at my bachelors' party at the Castle. All the fellows on the casino floor knew there was something crazy going on with her running the Castle and Ivana's pay scale. Everyone on the casino floor was speculating about what they thought was going on.

The rumors of her husband Donald's infidelity were floating around on the casino floor, which means there could only be one reason for Ivana Trump to be in this position. *Pussy!* Ivana had no idea about the daily casino operations, instead she spent her time annoying the hotel employees, bathroom attendees. If Ivana did walk on the casino floor, trust and believe it was only to show off her new outfit, because she was clueless about the workings of table games.

Things started getting a little crazy around the Castle. There was talk of my man Bucky, the vice president of operations, getting indicted for taking kickbacks, things were falling apart at the Trump Castle. I recall this one day my crap table was so hot you couldn't help but win money. It was cool because it was great for publicity, the sixteen players on that table were partying and having a payday. Whenever people win, they would go back and tell their friends, cousins, family members, and that's how you established new clientele, word of mouth is everything. No matter what you did you were making money on this roll. The dice wouldn't stop. Everybody was screaming and shouting and having a good time.

People were stopping trying to see what was happening on the table, the action was very heavy. Lots of my clients came down to Atlantic City from Staten Island, Long Island, Connecticut, Manhattan, Alabama, Cali, Ohio, all over the world for that one reason. They knew my game would be hot with plenty of action, and they were going to have a great time on my table.

February 22nd, 1987, was a good day for gamblers on my crap table until I noticed some railbirds. I tried not to be obvious or alarm any of my players, but a railbird is someone who stands by you or behind you and tries to reach under your arm and grab a few chips.

It didn't matter who it was, it could've had Mike Tyson on my table, the heavyweight champion of the world. I still had to put their safety first and wouldn't expect anyone to have to fight. So, I reported my suspicions to the pit boss manager, Carol, and kept it moving. It was out of my hands now.

The pit boss called up surveillance causing the lights to get brighter on the crap table, they also had security sent down to the game. Suddenly, you could feel the tension in the area around the crap table with these two old ass security guards standing in the back of the crap table with their radio in their hands. I had no reason to feel uncomfortable or be afraid, security was there, I didn't know these men. It's not like they were even gambling, I couldn't care less about these railbirds.

Let security handle it, I have to run a crap game, and this was common in Atlantic City. If you were not careful or have someone watching your back, that could be a bad thing in this city. You can easily become a victim. We had some real professional criminals and pickpockets came from all over the world! I still had a job to do and either the two old ass security guards who were looking like Barney Fife from the *Andy Griffin Show* or the railbird fools that were making the whole table feel uncomfortable.

One of the high rollers pointed to his mouth and his watch, I knew what that meant he was hungry and wanted his comp. It was never polite to shout out a client's business across the table. You had to give them that respect, face-to-face, and shake their hand. I couldn't allow myself to be intimidated by anyone as the dice game goes on, let's get a roll.

As I walked out of the pit with a comp, pen, and pad to give my player his comp and take another rating from a different client, the biggest man was getting a little too close to me. I continued talking to my player, security didn't budge. The little old security guard just looked at me as if to let me know that he had my back, but he was still behind the table.

As I continued talking, the largest of the potential assailants began to move even closer to me and began calling me names because security was making them feel very uncomfortable by watching them. He shouted, "You called security on us, pussy?" I looked at the security guards, and not one of them even attempted to come out of the pit. So, I ignored the man and continued the conversation with the player.

Finally, he made it a point to get in my face and let me know that he was mad at me for having security there. He called me a pussy for the second time. He said, "You're a pussy for calling security on us!" I could see out of the corner of my eye that security still wasn't moving at all. This man never should have been allowed to get this close to me, after all, security was here. Although this man was twice my size, I had to be ready because he was in my face while security still just stood there looking. I must admit, this was one big motherfucka, but I wasn't letting anyone stop me from doing my job, the players and dealers began to shout at the security guards, "Go out there and do your job!"

At that point, I knew I was on my own. Again, the big man said, "You're a pussy!"

"I'm not going to be, too many of them pussies, sir." Then bam, he punches me *Straight to my left eye*! I fell back eight feet into a little old lady sitting at the blackjack table. She broke my fall; I knew I crashed into her hard as hell. I could see the blackjack table on its side out of the corner of my eye. Realizing that I was still conscious and standing after taking his best shot, it was time for me to take action. Yelling at him, *"Welcome to Brooklyn, motherfucka, and you hit like a bitch!"* Then I went directly into that ass with a flurry of lefts and rights and backed his ass up to the crap table. He grabbed my suit jacket and pulled it over my back to try and lock my arms up. I came out of the jacket with him holding it in his hands, got a few more lefts and rights in before I felt someone jumping on my back knocking me to the floor.

Laying there with a lot of pressure on my back and someone's fingers in my eyes, I couldn't believe that I was being jumped on the casino floor. In order to be able to identify the person on my back as he was putting his fingers in my eyes, that baby pinky of his was right by my mouth. Knowing that I couldn't see this motherfucka's face, I damn sure wanted to be able to identify his ass, one way or another. I bit that mothafucka's pinky like it was a White House sub sandwich! Having no idea how many people were on my back, just feeling the pressure, someone shout out, "That's Cutty out there, that's Cutty out there." Before I knew it, the weight was getting lighter and lighter on my back and punches being thrown. It sounded like an all-out brawl as a matter of fact it was.

It turned out that my coworkers Dominic, Big Posey and Big Isgro, had come to my aid. As I got up, there was total chaos and pandemonium. On the next crap table down, there was a dealer standing on top screaming her brains out and the crap table that I had the man against was standing on half of its legs with the other half on the floor. After more guards, the DGE, and police officers arrived order was restored.

Someone tossed me my shoe as the pit boss Carol, walked me back in the pit and made me sit down. Sitting on a stool in the pit by the crap table, I realized that my watch was missing, the floor was flooded with security guards and Atlantic City police officers. I looked up toward the catwalk in the mirrors and saw that my eye was swollen, as I sat there it really began bothering me.

Not knowing any of these men, they could have done whatever they wanted, except put their hands on me. There was still a need to be able to identify the big guy who sucker punched me in the eye. All I knew was that he was a big ass mothafucka with glasses on. I got up out of my chair with one shoe in my hand and the other one on my foot, this shit really bothered me. Shoe back on, I couldn't stop thinking about this piece of shit. He had no right to touch me, clearly a bully and I down right despise bullies. Unfortunately, he had no idea that this little motheafucka was from Bed-Stuy, and he fucked up by not knocking me out.

I'm just getting started now. This shit isn't over. Walking by my Italian boys, Dominic, Big Bryon and Big Isgro who had their jackets off with their sleeves rolled up, acting like everything was cool and I was going to let security and the police handle it from this point on, it's under control.

When I saw that piece of shit over there between two crap tables talking to the police, one of my coworkers George, look me in my eye and shook his head. Knowing my eye was bad didn't matter it was still on. The police were pulling their cuffs out, walking slowly and coolly, without anyone being alarmed, not believing that they literally let me get so close. Maybe they didn't see me being close enough to plant my left foot and from there I gave him 185 pounds of pure power with my right fist and 450 pounds of torque power straight through his glasses. This man needed to remember me for the rest of his life. His right eye was a clean target with glasses on. My right hand hit his eye causing it to explode with blood shooting from it as both of his knees buckled in front of me.

Watching him slam one guard against the crap table, I felt like Iron Mike Tyson. Staring at him while walking away in slow motion felt like I was going back to my corner. The whole crowd went into an uproar cheering, screaming, and clapping. Surely, he remembers this little man from Brooklyn for a long time to come.

After being escorted down to the nurse's office to get my eye looked at by the house doctor, while sitting in the nurse's office all the casino management came down to check on me. Then being told that the man said I step on his foot, so he hit me. I asked one of the managers if they could get my friend McDuffie to come down there.

As the managers all walked out, I heard the doctor telling someone in the next examining room, "That finger needs to be stitched together, or you're going to lose it." There was only a curtain dividing us, knowing that this had to be that other man and that this was probably my last chance to engage with him, it was time to act. Raising quietly, walked over to the curtains, peeking to see where he was. Once the curtains opened all the way, it was time to take it right to him before he could figure out what hit him. Doing my James Brown count down silently. 1, 2, 1, 2, 3 Hit it! Then he sensed the curtains being pulling back, turned around and caught my same powerful right "Bammm!" straight to his face. As he flew into the doctor's workstation, he was caught by a few more of those powerful rights. Then a metal tray, that the doctor had bandages on that he was going to use to wrap the man's finger, was in my hands hitting him in the head a few times. The metal tray was making the oddest sounds, *bong, pong, bong*, each time it hit him in his head. "You like jumping people don't you, you fucking coward!" *Bamm!* the tray found its target again. Security finally arrived with my man McDuffie. They grabbed the tray and broke up the fight, the switch was still on *Fuck it, who's next!* not sure if it was two or three left, still good to go now and ready to continue rumbling.

Shortly after being evaluated, they transported me to Atlantic City Medical Center. That's where they gave me a series of CT scans and x-rays.

After taking some time off, returning to work with warm wishes from coworkers and other managers, it became a daily reminder by the security guards of the fight. It was impossible to sit down without a security guard wanting to meet me or shake my hand. While eating lunch, a big ass guard walked up to my table, sat down, and said, "Do you know how many times a day your name comes up about that fight?"

"Yeah, I can imagine!"

"I wish I was there!"

"Why is that?"

"Because I would've been right out there rumbling with you."

"So where were you that day?"

"Oh! I wasn't working here then."

"So how do you know about the fight?"

"I saw a tape of the event in a training class."

The surveillance tape had become part of a training program for security and others. As time went by one day came when Mrs. Trump met me by chance walking to the employee cafeteria. Her two security guards both knew me, so they allowed us to talk. Introducing myself she knew immediately who I was and became very apologetic saying, "Yes, I saw the videotape, and that should have never gotten that far!"

"I agree."

"But if you have any problems, you come to my office right away to see me. By the way, you're a great fighter"

"Thanks Mrs. Trump." and that was that.

That single punch on the casino floor to the big man's

eye became known as the punch that was heard around the Castle. Still remembering this man's knees buckling, it took Ivana Trump and the director of human resources almost a year just to get approval to pay for the Giorgio Armani suit and tie I was wearing at the time of the fight. Becoming overwhelmed with the bullshit from the personnel department, this short fat fuck Ed, who oversaw human resources, really felt he could say anything to an employee and get away with it. As things became increasingly uncomfortable, keeping my distance from this piece of shit seemed to be a good idea. Ed couldn't believe a person could pay decent money for a suit and tie.

Continuingly being approached by different security guards with dumb ass questions about the fight was becoming a problem. One security guard ask me, "Where did you learn how to fight?"

The Fallout:My Brooklyn Instincts!!

After retaining one of the best lawyers in Atlantic City, Mr. Spitassnah, and on November 13, 1987, he sent a letter to Trump Castle demanding a copy of the tape. Within two weeks of the dated demand letter for the tape, the personnel department called me in. After waiting for some time for that fat fuck, Ed, the head of human resource, to come out of his office he finally appeared. However, Ed wasn't aware of my own investigation into his background, he came out of his office with my files in his hand and took a seat. He pulled out my application and said, "Trump Castle is terminated your employment because of falsifying your employment application."

"Really"

"Yes, you failed to disclose that you were terminated from Caesar's hotel and casino eight years ago on your application."

"Number one, why would anyone put something derogatory like that on their application? Not to mention at the time all that was really needed on any employment application at Trump Castle was one's birth date, social security number, a signature and they hired me. Be honest with me Mr. Ed, is this termination letter is really about what I didn't mention on my application?"

"Yes!"

"Because the Trump personnel department has a letter dated exactly two weeks ago from today from my lawyers, asking the Trump organization to make arrangements to view the videotape of the fight, or provide us with a copy of it."

"THERE IS NO TAPE!"

"Since we're talking about things that weren't disclosed on my application, did you put on your application that you were terminated from Harrah's Hotel casino for your sexual harassment against Mrs. DeAmbroshore?"

The room became totally quiet as Ed began to change colors clearly a nerve was hit. Someone needed to tell this fat fuck to breathe. He turned red and blue then the four foot 380-pound asshole began asking, "Can I have your ID?"

"I'll surrender my ID when I pick up my last paycheck."

After walking out of the personnel department, taking the escalators down and leaving the building, once home and still annoyed, it was time to give Mrs. Ivana Trump's office a call. Ivana wasn't available, so they connected me to her personal secretary, Ms. Paige, it went like this, "Hello, Ms. Paige, my name is Stevie G, and Mrs. Trump told me to call if I ever had any problems."

"You're the gentleman that was involved in the fight, correct?"

"Yes, ma'am."

"Well, what can I do or tell Ms. Trump for you?"

"You can tell her that I was terminated today from my employment with Trump Castle, and I would like to surrender my ID badge to her or you, and if she wants me to have my job back, she can contact me."

"Okay! I'll be more than ready to accept your ID back."

"I would like to surrender my ID into her office so she's aware of the situation."

"Well, Ms. Trump will be in meetings the rest of the day, but if you want to come down to the VIP office and ask for me, Paige, I will be glad to take your ID from you, and I'll make sure that Ms. Trump gets your message."

"What's a good time to come down to your office, Ms. Paige?"

"Let's make it for one-thirty in the afternoon tomorrow."

"Thanks, Ms. Paige, and I'll see you tomorrow at 1:30 p.m."

The following morning while speaking with the personnel department, they advised me that my check was ready. Having had a good night's rest and blessed to see another day, decided to wear something nice in anticipation of saying my goodbyes to coworkers and friends. Still not believing what was happening, if Ivana wanted me to have my job back, she'd let me know.

After walking into the VIP office, giving the secretary my name, asking to see Ms. Paige, she asked me to have a seat. Two- or three-minutes past, four or five security guards entered the main reception area, all of them started pointing at me and then said, "Stand up, come with us, stand up, stand up!"

Once standing, tackled from the back, pushed to the floor, handcuffed, while a few ladies there watched, these guards came prepared to hurt me and did just that. One of the guards twisted the cuffs to hurt my wrists and made sure the cuffs were extra-tight there had to be at least eight hands on me. The security guards were pinching, pulling, pushing me, and everyone was shouting. It seemed like everyone wanted to get a chance to hurt me any way they could.

They escorted me upstairs in Trump Castle to the security office where they had a holding cell. Some of the guards were really really trying to provoke me. Being outnumbered by the guards, a few of them clearly wanted to prove to some of the older guards that they were tough. By not feeding into their tactics, they had no reason to really hurt me. While cooperating with the guards one of them asked me a stupid ass question, "What's your name?"

"My full name?"

"Yes!"

"Turn around! Do you see that flyer on the wall?"

"Yes."

"Well, that's me!"

"Oh!"

"Are you that stupid? My pictures are all over this office, like Trump Castle's most wanted, with my name on them."

Those pictures had to have been taken the day before because of the clothes I had on in them. Finally, an Atlantic City police officer came into the office. All the security guards ran over to him and started telling him their stories, it seemed like they all wanted to be the police officer's hero. The police officer asked me, "What's your name, sir?"

"My name is Stevie G, and your name, Officer?"

"My name is Officer Tibbs, and I'm going to be transporting you to the Atlantic City Police Station."

All the security guards began to shout to the officer saying what they did to take me into custody, laughing and pointing at me. After asking Officer Tibbs, "Do you know Officer Kellum, a.k.a. Boom boom, or the V-Brothers, Joe and Greg, or Ralph the Mouth?"

"I know all of them guys. I just saw Joe V three days ago."

"Well, look, can you do them a favor, and I promise you them guys will thank you!"

"What's the favor?"

"Don't let any of these punk ass guards put their hands on me."

"Don't worry buddy, no one is going to touch you, how do you know them guys?"

"I was there when they first started walking their beat on Atlantic Avenue by Creamers Supermarket."

"Wow, I remember that beat."

"Joe V taught me how to make a fist that will take the wind out of a person with a punch. I guarantee you when you see those guys, they will thank you for looking out for me."

"You're going to be just fine, and no one's going to do anything to you."

"Thanks, Officer Tibbs. Oh, one more thing, Officer Tibbs, can you loosen up these cuffs just a little? One of the guards was twisting my wrist as we were walking."

"Someone give me your KEY!"

"Here!"

"Thanks! After they complete their paperwork, I'll have you out of here soon, my friend!"

"Thanks Officer Tibbs!"

Finally, after being taken downstairs to an awaiting police car and being transported to the Atlantic City Police Station, sitting in my cell it hit me. *This was the first time in my life being handcuffed and arrested.* Alone in the cell this fact hit me hard, I was hurt and devastated.

Though I've done many crazy things in my life, living in Brooklyn, New York, Chester, Pennsylvania, North Philly, Atlantic City, never been arrested and handcuffed in my life. Now feeling broken as a man, this really mess me up, locked up by a confused millionaire wife who's pissed off with her husband.

Mad at myself for trusting this woman, because knowing when to back up without getting into trouble or arrested was normal for me. My parents taught me excellent instincts during earlier in life in Brooklyn. Clearly my talents were no longer needed at the Castle.

After being released with charges pending, assaulting three security guards, trespassing, and more, my thoughts turned to losing my casino license. Confused and in need of advice I reached out to one of the V brothers, Joe. He said, "If you don't have any witnesses that can say you were told to come down there, you may be going to jail because all the guards are going to stick together. So, get someone or some type of proof, by law, tapes are inadmissible in court unless both parties are aware of it, and stay out of trouble."

"Thanks, Joe!"

Once home, after pacing back and forth for some time, realization for the first time hit, I was stuck and didn't know what to do! All kinds of things were going through my head. Couldn't believe that going to jail was a real possibility. Evidence of being invited to the VIP office the day before would be critical to my staying out of jail. On top of all that my wife still had no idea about any of this. My thoughts returned Joe V's advice.

A trip to Radio Shack where a small tape recorder with an attachment for a phone receiver, was purchased in my effort to get Ivana Trump's secretary, Ms. Paige, on tape. The call was made just before four-thirty. Once on the phone, I identified myself and asked her, "What happened?"

"When I came out of my office to get the ID from you, all I saw was a bunch of security guards on top of you on the floor. The guards pushed me back in my office!"

"Why didn't you tell them that you were expecting me?"

"I did, I told them you were to come down here to surrender your ID to me at one-thirty. I even showed them the appointment on my calendar desk pad."

"Well, they roughed me up, but did Mrs. Trump ever get my ID?"

"No, she didn't!"

"Well, is there any way that you can tell Mrs. Trump that you told me to come down there so they can drop the charges on me?"

"I did tell Mrs. Trump that, but security told me to say that you need to direct all your questions to the lawyers from now on!"

"Thanks, Ms. Paige, and happy Thanksgiving to you and your family." At this point the decision was made in my mind that a message needed to be delivered. When, how, or who didn't matter. One day Ivana Trump was going to know that not keeping her word to me was not appreciated, at all.

More Lawyers get Involved, Still no fun!!

Retaining one of the toughest lawyers in New Jersey, ball head Harry G., he took the tape and listened to it. He was a little annoyed because it was more of my voice than Paige's voice, but it was enough for Harry G. to tell the Trump organization to bring what they had to court. Everything that could be done to avoid going to jail or lose my casino license, was being done.

There was still a focus on delivering my message to Ivana Trump. It wasn't about my job or money; it was her word that my believing in caused all the problems. Hoping Ivana would intervene and tell whoever was in charge to drop the charges for the three security guards that said I assaulted them. Their tactic was very simple delay, delay, delay, with no answer in sight. It was time to start looking for a lawyer that could get this thing going and match my passion to win.

Harry knew my emotional state, but it was just business for him. Sad to say, it had become personal for me. So, Harry was dropped. I was ready to go to war. Feeling that without a

36

good fight and standing up tall for myself, Donald wouldn't respect me, let's fight!

Not being able to stop thinking about being handcuffed, my attitude was growing increasingly worse. Vindication for me would be nice but having my message delivered by someone who was close to Ivana would be great. Her not keeping her word was wrong and mess up.

Day after day my attitude continued to deteriorate. Always thinking about who would be best to tell this woman about my anger, was not helpful. Not knowing whether jail was in my future, it started not to matter anymore. Fuck it! My attitude was becoming harder and rougher and if going to jail was in my future, it would be for a reason. After going through several different lawyers and literally snatching my files out of one of the lawyers' hands, it was time for a change.

Apparently, what was needed was a lawyer who didn't have a problem standing up to the Trumps, instead of making me feel that they wanted to work for them. Also needed was a lawyer that didn't have a problem with me fighting along with him. Knowing that's crazy, didn't trusting any lawyers, I still couldn't back down.

One lawyer that may have been able to handle the case was Mr. Bromley from Atlantic City. Unfortunately, he didn't want anything to do with the case because it had been through too many other lawyers' hands already. He felt that the case was contaminated.

The search moved to central New Jersey, where one Lawrence Hecker, was identified. He didn't work out because he wasn't mad enough. Moving the search up to North Jersey one Robert Clark was engaged. Making it clear to him that it was time for me to get back on my feet, he was good to go. I'd been sitting around feeling sorry for myself for way too long.

It took a lot to stand up for what I believed in. Eventually, I'll get back to Trump and his wife Ivana. Donald Trump himself always said that if you believe in something with all your heart and soul, you fight for it tooth and nail! One day Donald Trump himself would deliver my message to his wife. For now, a new job was needed to bring in some type of income to support my family, and this job was needed quickly!

Going back into the casino life anytime soon was not an option. Mrs. Trump's betrayal really had me in a negative state of mind. A high price was paid and continued to be paid! A hated night job that paid the bills was finally secured.

On December 13, 1991, Robert Clark was sent a letter demanding my file. It's been some time since hearing from him. Believing that my suspicions were pretty much on point after he did not return my calls, he was a piece-of-shit. No money or apology, just my file back and we would be straight.

Calling Clark's office telling him my name was Tyrone Green, who had been on a New Jersey Transit bus when it was hit by a limo. Further my grandmother asked me to call, his secretary kindly made an appointment for me. Going up there on the appointment day with a friend, Curtis, entered Clark's office, Curtis sat in the car while Clark's secretary greeted me. After telling her my name and about my appointment with Mr. Clark, his secretary went back into his office. Looking over everything on her desk and on the floor, my files were finally spotted.

He came out of his office, looked at me, then walked back into his office. Coming back with his receptionist, he looked at me, turned pale, began to stutter, looked at her and said, "That's not Tyrone Green, who I was expecting, his name is Mr. G. and not at all expecting him!"

"Well, while am I here, I need to pick up my file!"

"Well, you should have called because your files are not ready yet."

"Well, I think they are ready now, as a matter of fact, they're so ready I have them in my briefcase!"

"If you walk out this office with that file, I'm going to call the police and say that you assaulted me and my secretary."

"If you touch that phone before I touched that doorknob, your secretary is going to be explaining what happened to your fat ass."

Closing the door, counted to three, then reopening the door, they were still standing there in disbelief. Closing the door, headed down the back steps, jumped in the car, and off we went. The police never came for me. My wife needed to know what had just happened in case the police did show up, but it just wasn't the right time.

After a few days of going through my files and discovering that the case was dismissed because Clark failed to attend an earlier conference hearing, it was clear what needed to happen next. For Christmas 1991, a letter to Judge Himmelberger Jr. asking him to reinstate my case was sent.

A few weeks later a letter from the NJ Supreme Court, Judge Himmelberger arrived. It advised me that my case had indeed been dismissed because of failure to appear. At that time Mr. Clark would have to file a motion to get it reinstated. After immediately calling Clark and telling his secretary to have her boss reinstate the case, nothing was heard from Clark for months.

Decided to visit Clark again at 645 Central Avenue, East Orange, New Jersey. Fortunately, things didn't go the way they had been planned, which in turn became the biggest blessing ever. Anger at Clark finally eased enough to ask myself who was my fight really with, Clark or Trump. This whole thing had become a little out of control and a need to bring closure to this chapter in my life was now clear.

Remembering at one point asking Mr. Clark, "If you get a chance, could you tell Ivana Trump that I didn't appreciate her not keeping her word?" He just laughed it off and said that he would be the man to do it! Knowing he was a piece of shit that day, but still needing my life back with my wife and kid. Determining that my feeling better could happen if some Trump glass was broken, it would at least release some stress. As long as all this misplaced aggression remained, my life couldn't move forward. Being able to make a few dollars to feed my family, had not removed the chip from my shoulder.

I'd catch myself thinking about being handcuffed to the wall and Ivana never attempted to right the wrong she had caused. My new night job didn't help my attitude. Tried to get my mother and father to understand my point of view without success. Still lost, my mother wanted me to put this situation in the Lord's hand. My father took the time and talked to me and said, "Son, I want you to pick and choose your battles!"

I replied, "I feel as if the Trumps were trying to keep things quiet, but she's trying to intimidate me with her power and lawyers with the fear of me going to jail."

"That should scare you, son!"

"It would if I had done something wrong, Dad!"

"Do you think you did something wrong, son?"

"No, not at all! The security guards use the fight tape as a training lesson."

"How do you know that son?"

"All day long I have security guards coming up to me asking me crazy questions about the fight!"

"Like what?"

"Was I ever a boxer, just stupid things. One of the guards came short of asking me for an autograph."

"Are you sure there's a tape, son?"

"Management said that there was no tape existing, but I still get asked questions like I'm a celebrity to all the new security guards, and there were certain things that I heard from some guards about the fight! That fit to a T. Either you had to be there or watch that tape."

"All this because you asked to see the tape?"

"Yes!"

"Did you ask for the tape or a lawyer, son?"

"The lawyer sent a letter to Trump's lawyer asking to see the tape and exactly two weeks later, after they received the letter, things went crazy, Pops. Two weeks later all because of pursuing the videotape, Pops."

"Son, people like the Trumps have enough money to put you in jail."

"If I go to jail for something that I believe in, I'm good!"

"You're still hardheaded son, your mom and I just want you to get your life back on track, son!"

"I feel as if she's using her power and lawyers!"

"What do you want from the Trumps, son?"

"To be honest, Pops, I'll settle for a lousy apology."

"I don't want you to waste your time waiting for an apology son, your life will be on hold, while their lawyers put you and your life on standby, son!"

"Do you think if Donald had someone send a note to his home in a demanding way, it would bother him enough to tell his wife what I said!"

"Which home, son, he's a millionaire?"

"I'll send him a note to his main home in New York City, Trump Towers!"

"If Donald Trump doesn't respond, will you get on with

your life, son?"

"Absolutely, Pops."

"Son, let me make it clear, I don't think you can win this fight."

"You're probably right, Dad. I'm not trying to win a fight. I just want to be heard. Donald Trump himself said if you believe in something, you fight for it tooth and nail, and I know if I just ignored this, Donald Trump himself wouldn't respect me either. I honestly believe in my heart I was unfairly treated!"

"I don't care what Donald Trump said. Look, son, I don't want anything to happen to you!"

"But to be locked up and handcuffed to a wall, knowing that I'm innocent, and that was my first time *ever* being locked up. Not to mention not knowing if you're going to jail or not. Something already has happened to your son, Pops. Shit like that can change the type of person you are, especially if you're innocent."

"I understand that son!"

"If I do something, I'm man enough to stand up and say I did it, isn't that how you raised me, Dad?"

"You're absolutely right, son."

"If I had a drug problem Dad, would you and Mom send

me away and get me help?"

"Absolutely! You're our son and we love you."

"Well, this is something I'm learning how to deal with day by day. Dad."

"I understand son."

"In New Jersey, if you get the wrong municipal ticket, the CCC, a.k.a. the Casino Control Commission, wants to have a hearing for a suspension or probably a cause to revoke your casino license."

"Son, sometimes you have to take it like a man and humble yourself."

"You're right, Pops, but in these days and time, you have to stand up for yourself. If I'm wrong, I'm wrong, right?"

"Right, son!"

"Now if I'm right, then I'm right, correct?"

"Yes, son!"

"I was taught that by you. If you don't stand for something, you will fall for anything."

"And you're right, son, but I don't want you to spend the rest of your life fighting these people, they're rich and can buy or get any lawyer you have on their side, just to prove a point, son."

"I know, Pops, but Ivana had plenty of time to stop all these shenanigans if she really didn't want me to go through this. Let's face it, every woman has a little crazy in them, it just takes the right asshole to bring it out of them. She could have said something or just made a phone call to stop me from thinking I was going to jail, but she chose to dog me, and that was really mess up."

"What do you want to happen, son?"

"I want a person that Ivana Trump will listen to and know, to tell her that I didn't appreciate her not keeping her word,"

My father burst out laughing. "Who are you going to get to tell . . ahhh ahhhh, what was her name?"

"Who?"

"Donald's wife?"

"Ivana!"

"Yes, Ivana! Who's going to tell her that?"

"Maybe I'll get her husband Donald, to tell her that!"

My father burst out laughing again and said, "That night

shift you're on has you missing too much sleep son!"

"After all Pops, he's the asshole who made her crazy?"

My dad burst out laughing again.

"Exactly Dad, her husband Donald made her ass crazy, so let him tell Ivana!"

"I don't know what I'm going to do with you, son!"

"Just continue loving me, Pops."

My father burst out laughing again and said, "You need to get off that night shift son, it's given you a bad attitude."

"I know, Pops. I'll get it together soon Pops."

"I hope so son."

"I will Pops, as soon as Donald Trump says he heard me loud and clear."

On January 8, 1992, Judge Himmelberger Jr. told me that the case was dismissed for failure to appear. Feeling in my heart that the Trump organization got to my lawyer, he sold his soul along with his practice. Well, it was time for Donald Trump's lawyers to get back in contact with this piece-of-shit lawyer Clark and ask for Donald's money back. I was going to make sure that Clark's name popped up in the Trump organization again, the best was yet to come.

Four Bricks in New York and the Message!

At the beginning of March 1992, while in the supermarket, waited in line, a tabloid magazine with Ivana and Donald Trump on the cover caught my eye. The picture looked like they wanted to kill each other or bite each other's head off. It's over, the Trumps were headed for Splits Ville, they're divorcing, and Ivana wanted half.

It was so sad, but the timing was perfect. Deciding to send the message to Donald Trump so he could deliver it to his soon-to-be ex-wife Ivana. Understand that Ivana was furious with her soon-to-be ex-husband, being sympathetic for her was not enough to let her take her fury out on me. Her poor treatment of me would not be ignored. Who's going to give that message to her? Her soon-to-be ex-husband, Donald. As always, I called up my best friend McDuffie, to see if he could do me a favor that night. "Yo, McDuffie, I need you to do me a big favor.

"You got it! What's the favor?"

"I need you to take me to the bus station tonight!"

"What bus station?"

"AC!"

"What time?"

"About 9:00 p.m."

"Is everything okay?"

"Yes! Why?"

"You're going to catch the bus to NYC in the middle of the night, and you have a car!"

"I know. I have to go to New York to take care of some business."

"Wussup, man? Do we need to talk?"

"Nah, I'm good. Just come and pick me up about 9:00 p.m. and we'll talk a little more."

"Cool, I'll see you then."

Still had time to get this little plastic bag that was given to the employees by Ivana Trump at the company's summer party. A plastic bag, white, with a strap on it and a Trump Castle logo on two sides. It was a plastic piece of shit able to hold four cans of cold beer or soda. It was also perfect for four eight-inch brown cement bricks. Just like it was made for them. Zipped up perfectly with the bricks inside.

My wife knew that something heavy on my mind, but not being happy about the fact that the whole situation was still bothering me it was best to just leave it alone for now. Instead, left my bag outside, went into the house and kissed her good night. Shortly we heard a horn blowing outside.

My wife asked, "Are you going to work tonight?"

"Maybe a little later, but right now I'm going to talk to McDuffie. Get some rest. I love you."

"I love you too. Be safe!" After walked out of the house, the first thing was to go around the side of the house and get my three joints of sinsemilla, the best marijuana in South Jersey, and put them up in a safe spot. *Now ready!* Grabbed my Trump Castle bag and put it in the back seat of McDuffie's car.

"Yo, wuss good, McDuffie?"

"I don't know, you tell me, you're the one who must go up to New York to handle some business on a late night, do we need to talk?"

"Nah I'm good. I just have to reach out and touch someone, that's all."

"Com-on, man, we took plenty of walks before!"

"I know."

"Are you sure you don't want to talk, man?"

"Nah, I'm good, but you can take me to the liquor store on Arkansas and Atlantic Ave."

"Yo, what's in that Trump Castle bag?"

"Some shit from my garden."

"I still got my bag lying around somewhere. I think I got screws and nails and shit in there."

"Cool!"

"So, what's in that bag again?"

"Nothing, man, just some things from the garden! Wait right here while I run in the store."

"Okay!"

In and out of the store then said to McDuffie, "Thanks my brother, just drop me off right in front of Greyhound bus station on Arctic Avenue."

"Okay!"

"I'll see you when I get back in town."

"Yo? Quick question?"

"Wussup?"

"Are you packing a piece in that bag?"

"Not at all!"

"Are you?"

"Yo man, if I needed to go somewhere packing, I would've let you know bruh, but I love you for being concerned about me. I'm cool homie, tap the bottom of this bottle for me."

"Yo damn, you got a whole pint of Brass Monkey?"

"I know."

"I haven't seen that shit in a while."

"I know right! But it gets you there. I used to get this before going to Franklinville roller rink or Empire Boulevard roller rink when I was younger."

"Yo, man, if I didn't have to go to work in the morning, I would ride up to New York with you."

"Nah, I'm cool. Besides, I have to go up there by myself anyway."

"All right, brother, are you sure you don't want to take a ride and talk for a minute?"

"I'm good my brother, I just have to hand deliver a message up there, via the bus."

"All right, all right, touch base with me as soon as you get back from New York!"

"Okay."

"Yo?"

"Wussup!"

"The things from the garden are heavy as shit."

"I know, good greens stay on your stomach longer."

"I'm just saying!"

"Yo, I'm good! I'm just taking some fresh greens and shit up there! I'll see you when I get back in town."

"I love you, brother!"

"And I love you back, my brother!"

Still had time to talk to McDuffie, knew he would have done whatever he could've to prevent me from getting in trouble or hurt. My mind was made up already! The only question left was where to send my message, the Plaza, the Castle, or Taj Mahal? All these places were in Atlantic City, which Trump rarely came to anymore. Going to Florida was out of the question, which narrowed it down to just two places.

The Plaza or Trump Towers in New York City would have to do. Either one would allow the message to be delivered. Truth of the matter is, if you want something done your way, then do it yourself! Conscious decision to go to Trump Towers in Manhattan made, this way Trump would see that it was personal.

Now with twenty minutes left before boarding the bus, sitting in the park across from the bus station between Arctic and Atlantic Avenues, there was still time to think this out thoroughly. Once on that bus there would be no turning back. This was my last chance to smoke a joint and think about the Trump situation in Atlantic City with this woman Ivana. It began to bother me again, that was my first time ever being handcuffed in my life! Not to mention that Ivana could've asked her secretary, Paige, to tell the truth. Instead, she chose to ignore it and off to jail I went. Fortunately, my conversation was recorded with Paige. During which she clearly stated that she told me to come to Ivana Trump's office. A good friend, one of Atlantic City's finest, told me straight up, "If you don't have proof that you were told to come down to her office, you're going to jail for a while." That was one of the worst feelings in the world, to have someone piss on your head and tell you that it's raining out or throwing shit on you just because their life sucks. "Guilty!" So, I did what I had to do to get proof, and that tape was what kept my ass out of jail. Another sip, still thinking about how this shit could've been avoided if one person had remained truthful to the game. Check the purse first and the ass last! Donald had become Donnie, he was thinking with his dick to put this crazy, scorned, psychopath, (another needs a sip) woman, who's mad at the world because he's dumping her ass for Marla. Who cares!

At the end of the day, it's only right to look out for my best friend, my black ass! A double sip this time, as the joint disappeared into the sky. Okay. it's time to catch the bus, let's take a sip for the bus, the bus driver, everyone who has a good pot, and anything else worth sipping too on the bus. Sitting on the bus, recalling a conversation that I had with my pops and him saying, "Son, I know that this Trump thing is really bothering you, but you have to pick and choose your battles."

"Just as I had explained to that piece-of-shit ex-attorney Robert B. Clark, I'm going to explain to you, Pop. When someone just feels as if they can shit on you and get away with it, that's not cool. If I'm wrong, I'm wrong. You know how you raised me, but if I'm right, and I feel I'm right beyond a reasonable doubt, I'm going to fight tooth and nail, and that's what Donald Trump said himself."

"YOU'RE NOT DONALD TRUMP, SON!"

"But I still deserve the same respect as a man, correct?"

"I understand son."

"I would've settled for an apology, but I have to let the

person know that there's a problem first. Is that correct, Pops?"

"I agree with you son, but these people don't care about you, so sometimes you have to move on and shake it off, son!"

"You're right, Pops, but if I had a problem with some type of substance abuse, I know that I can count on you and Mom for help, right?"

"Right, son!"

"But this right here left a nasty taste in my mouth, and mouthwash isn't working. I just need a little more time Pops, and I'm sure I'll feel better afterward. I know faith can move mountains, and Mom wants me to leave it alone and have faith in God to handle things, and prayer works. I know prayer works, but this has become personal. Ivana personally gave me her word out of her own mouth. It's up to me to let someone know if I have a problem with them and right now there's a problem with this woman. Even if I must be a one-man protester, I know no one in my family would approve or condone what I feel or think, but I had something on my chest, and I wasn't going to carry this shit anymore."

Feeling this way continued pushing me to get my message to Ivana. If my message was given to the right person, it would get relayed to Ivana. If only one person saw my message being delivered, they'll tell the police, Donald and Ivana Trump, the doorman, the elevator man, the custodian, the valet check man, the cameraman, and everyone else they could think of.

After taking a good nap, rested, still drunk not to mention hungry, reaching Port Authority, first thing was to get myself two chicken shish kabobs with some bread, barbecue sauce, and a Pepsi. Then walked toward Fifty-Fifth street with my Walkman and my bag of "garden stuff."

Finishing up my food and drink, still had time to smoke another joint. With two left, started puffing on one of them, put the last one under my foot in my sock for the after-party. There was no doubt in my mind that there was no backing down now. It felt good being in New York City listening to DJ Kid Capri (Cypress Hill, "Hand on the Pump)" on the walkman.

Shit, my stomach was full, feeling no pain, once my message was delivered using those items from the garden, everything would be straight. But right now, this brass monkey was working overtime, it was a beautiful night to be in NYC and it's going down now.

It's about to be a hellofva night, only one block away from my destination the closer, the harder and faster my heart pumped. Glad to have picked this property because it felt so very personal. Anywhere else wouldn't have been as effective a place to deliver my message.

Maybe it was the hook and the hard beat. The loop and the hook kept running over and over, over (Here is something you can't understand— "How I Could Just Kill a Man" by Cypress Hill). Knowing and feeling that it was about to be a hell of a night, there was no time for sightseeing. Time to deliver my message! Absolutely refusing to leave this city without fulfilling my goal, knowing there would be four chances to knock on the door.

Finally made it to my destination, standing in front of Trump Towers, smoking a joint and drunk as hell. Sitting down, my Trump bag with the zipper unzipped, the top was still covered. A security guard was leaning on a podium with his legs crossed while he was on the phone. This guy just looked too cool, smiling on the phone just chilling, so he was nominated to tell my story from this point on.

Looking at the glass revolving doors, which were very nice and a nice size too, but the door could be temporarily fixed with two boards tonight so nope, that's not it. Then checking out the glass to the left of the door, it's really a good size too. Once finishing up my joint, another no go decision was reached. This window could be covered up with maybe eight boards. Needing to let Donald know what the message was here tonight, the solution hit me. Laughing out loud, coming up for air there was my answer. Open to the public, way above the front doors, it was clear that this piece of glass wasn't going to be an easy fix.

Smashing it would allow time for some of the chilly ass New York City air and manhole cover smoke to run through the building and up the elevator shafts for a while. Still laughing hard, now the security guard was laughing on the phone to whomever he was talking to. This was making me laugh even more and soon we were both drying our eyes with our hands.

Okay, okay, getting a grip on things, still smiling with my wet eyes, time to focus on that big ass piece of glass. It was one solid piece. Knowing for a fact that if this glass needed replacing it was not going to go unnoticed for a day or two. It really looked like a special-order big ass piece of old thick glass.

As another short fat security guard emerged from behind a door, we all started laughing. The security guards were looking like Abbott and Costello. After leaning down, flipping open the lid of the bag, removing a brick and bounced it up and down in my hand, that Bugs Bunny song, "Powerhouse," was playing in my head.

The guard, who was there originally, was slowly take the smile off his face and put his hand up toward his eyes to block the glare of the light. He was making sure he was seeing what he thought he was seeing. The other fat guard was slowing his laughter as he grabbed the phone and started dialing. Two other guards came off the elevator as the whole lobby filled up with guards.

Fuck it, the guards all began to put their arms in the air and crossed them from side to side. Then the first brick was on its way, travel hard and fast as hell, Bamm! By then all the security guards looked like they were in a jumping jack class.

The brick bounced off the glass as if it was shatterproof. Guards were jumping up and down, looking like everyone in the breezeway was in an exercise class. Unbelievably, the brick didn't break this glass. Grabbing another one and giving it a full-throttle throw, this time the brick itself broke up into pieces while a little panic began to set in, the brick disintegrated.

This window had to break; brick number three had to be the one. The bricks were making echo sounds like JURASSIC PARK when they were hitting the glass. Throwing it with all my might it bounced off the glass again, it was as if the glass was made of plexiglass. Not to mention this was one of the biggest windows I'd ever seen.

Unbelievably this shit wouldn't break. Oh yeah, going to jail at this point was a certainty! Hearing police sirens getting closer and closer, there was only one brick left. Looking at the guards through the window, they were all still doing the exercise, crossing legs and arms, and jumping up and down. It even looked like some tenants and the elevator men joined in. The scene made the Kris Kross song, "Jump Jump" come to mind. If you had ridden down Fifty-Fifth street at this point, it would've looked like a live exercise class. Still, no one came out of the front door, maybe they weren't sure if other weapons were involved or not. Because everyone was just standing inside watching, they had a clear view of me taking the last brick, kissing it, then winding up to launch it just like Bugs Bunny.

Starting to laugh while winding the brick in a circle, just as sure as my ass was going to jail, this glass was going to break. Once the brick was on its way, I shouted out the words "Break!" Bammmm! *Crash!* And there it was. It finally caved in.

This was one of the prettiest things I'd ever seen, everyone stopped and looked up, just stirred as the glass was coming down in slow motion. It looked like a chandelier that was just cleaned or a scoopful of diamonds with a bright light on them. No one dared to move, instead we all just continued looking up, even when the glass stopped falling for a second.

There was one piece of glass still left just hanging. We all continued looking up waiting, waiting, and waiting for it to fall. It took forever, but everyone looked on and finally, it came down. Crash! And there it was, it was all over, and we were all eye to eye. One word was heard being yelled, "Getemmm!" After trying to pick up my little white bag, my Walkman dropped, picked it up but it dropped again. Stopped to put my headphones back on then realizes, *Ahhhshit, time for me to go.*

Running like a damn track star down Fifty-Fifth street toward Fifth Avenue, started feeling the liquor getting stronger, me getting drunker, then a cab appeared at the light on Fifth Avenue. Not being able to stop laughing, just continuing to run down toward Fifth Avenue. Finally stopped in my tracks, threw my hand up in the air and shouted out, "Taxi!" to hail the cab. For once in my life the cab stopped! The taxi remained at the light waiting for me, which made me laugh even harder.

Knowing the cab driver had seen all these guards chasing me, he still waited. Jumped in the back seat, closed the door, then the cab's back door lock goes *click!* The cab driver jumped out, while the guards gathered around the cab and got on their phones and walkie-talkies.

The one chubby guard who came down was laughing with the original guard and leaning on my back-door window trying to catch his breath. Rolling down the window a little and tapped the guard on his back, he took off running shouting "He has a gun!" Fortunately, the guard who was to tell the story remained by the cab. Signaling him to come over, when he did, I said, "Yo, my man? I don't have no gun on me."

"You sure?"

"I'm positive!"

"Okay!"

"Do you have a pen and a pad?"

"Yes!"

"Look, I need you to write this message down for me!"

"Okay!"

"Are you ready?"

"Yes!"

"Yo? I can use a match, if you have one, or a lighter?"

"Here you go!"

"So, when your boss Donald summons you to the executive office, here's what I want you to tell him!"

"Okay!"

"What's your name?"

"Rick!"

"Cool."

"What's the message?"

"Tell him that, the little Blackman from Brooklyn stopped by!"

"Okay!"

"And I need him!"

"Who's him?"

"Your boss Donald Trump, to tell her."

"Who's her?"

"His wife Ivana Trump."

"Okay!"

"I didn't appreciate her."

"Who's her?"

"His soon-to-be ex-wife Ivana Trump, that I didn't appreciate the bitch not keeping her word! Okay!"

"And where are you from?"

"Atlantic City!"

"And I guess you used to work under Ivana at Trump Castle in AC."

"Yeah, now you're cooking."

"Sorry, I got the bag over there."

"Cool! Security Rick?"

"Yes!"

"Here's one of my cards. If you ever come down to Atlantic City, look me up, I'm the driver."

"Cool!"

"I'll show you a good time, or you can give it to your boss Donald and tell him I said to relay my message to his wife."

"Okay!"

"If he wants to call me, give him my card."

"Okay!"

"Tell Donald if he doesn't give Ivana my message, fuck his window!"

"I can't say that I work for him!"

"Well, I don't, so put that shit in the report!"

"Okay!"

"And when you read the report to your boss, read it with a little attitude." He burst out laughing.

"Hey, Security Rick?"

"Yes!"

"That light show was awesome, wasn't it?"

"I've never seen anything like it, sir!" He started laughing again.

"So, you came all the way down from Atlantic City to deliver   this   message?" "Yelp! Do you think it's going to get delivered?"   "If you would have broken the door, I would say no. Even if you would have broken the glass next to the door, I would still say nope. But the glass that you broke is going to take some special attention."

"Cool, that was my exclamation mark!"   "Okay!"

"You can use that for your report and give a copy to Donald, Ivana and his next wife too!"

Talking with NYPD, and the Godfather!

Here comes New York's finest. Sitting in the cab smoking a cigarette watching the cops talk to the security guards, one of the cops started laughing. Couldn't hear the conversation, but sure it was about me. Glad that there had been no fighting with any of the security guards, still drunk as hell, laughing in the cab again, finally one of the police officers came over to the cab and introduced himself as Officer Russo who said, "How are you doing, sir?"

"I'm drunk Officer, but other than that, just fine!"

"All right, do you have any weapons on you, sir?"

"Nope!"

"Okay, I'm going to put you in the police car now."

"Thank you, sir!"

"After we get the guards' story, we'll be back to talk to you."

"Okay!"

"Then we're going to take you downtown to intake, and they'll take a statement and then process you there."

"Okay!"

"If the window costs more than $2,500, they may just keep you on the island until you make bail, or the judge may decide to release you on R&R and give you a summons with a court date."

"Okay."

"Was that security guard's statement pretty accurate, sir?"

"Did I use the word *bitch* in it?"

"Yes, sir."

"Then it's absofuckinlutely correct, Officer."

"Okay, just sit here in the squad car right now, and we'll

ride around to the front of Trump Towers to see what this is all about!"

"I can tell you what it's about!"

"What is it about?"

"It's about dice, lies, and video tape!"

"And you came all the way down from Atlantic City?"

"Yes, sir Officer, can you do me a small favor Officer?" He started laughing.

"What's the favor?"

"Can you please turn the radio dial to 107.5 WBLS for me?" He started laughing again. "Sure!"

As the officers and the guards exchanged notes outside, the damage done by the fourth brick became clear. Thinking about how beautiful it had been coming down, listening to WBLS playing, *"Living in the life"* by Karen Wheeler, started laughing my ass off in the back of the police car. That was a big ass piece of glass! No matter what anyone said everything felt great, since my message was going to get delivered to Donald. Hopefully, someone would bring this night up twenty-five years from now on Thanksgiving at the Trumps' dinner table while everyone was eating. On my way to Rikers Island, so what, nothing matter now that my message was on its way!

Somewhere down the road, remembering this night and laughing my ass off all over again, it would all be good. One day that police statement was going to come up, but it's cool because every single word of it was true. There's an old saying, "Say what you mean, and mean what you say!" Looking up at that big empty space in the front of Trump Tower, it came to me again that my message had been delivered. At that moment everything was good to go, the fight was all gone from me.

The other police officer came up and introduced himself as Officer Murphy, they both got back into the police car with Officer Murphy sitting in the driver's seat said, "Okay! So, you came all the way down from Atlantic City with four bricks in a Trump bag?"

"Correct!"

"And the report states that you came down to Trump Towers to deliver this message, right?"

"Yes, sir!"

"Have you tried to call or email Mr. Trump or his wife or soon-to-be ex-wife?"

"Yes, sir, his secretary, Heather, has plenty of my messages."

"So, who was the message actually for? Donald Trump or his estranged wife Ivana Trump?"

"The message was for his soon-to-be ex-wife Ivana?"

"So how did Donald Trump in New York City get involved in the picture?"

"I couldn't find anyone else to deliver my message to her."

"Okay!"

"Officer Murphy, I looked all over I even talked to a few lawyers, but no one had the balls to deliver my message to Ivana. So, who would've been a better candidate than the man who knows this woman firsthand and is also tired of her ass!"

"Who?"

"Besides me, her soon-to-be ex-husband."

"Donald!"

"Yes sir, now you're cooking!"

"And you did try to call up first?"

"Yes sir! I spoke to Norma and Geraldine."

"Okay!"

"Donald and Ivana are no longer together, right?"

"Correct!"

"And they're getting a divorce as we speak, right?"

"Correct!"

"I don't think they even like each other anymore!"

"Correct!"

"So, you came from Atlantic City with this Trump bag with four bricks in it, right?"

"Correct!"

"Let me get this right!"

"Okay!"

"Your purpose for breaking the glass was to deliver a message, right?"

"Almost right!"

"Well, what am I missing?"

"*Big ass glass* is what's missing!"

"That's another question, why that big ass glass?"

"Because I didn't want to annoy Donald with the door."

"What do you mean with the door?"

"If I would've broken the door, they would have put two boards up to it and repaired it. But a glass this size gives the staff, penthouse owners, maintenance men, tourists, visitors, old and new ass friends, and family members a chance to ask questions about that big ass window."

"Okay!"

"I needed for it to be a long day at Trump Towers the next morning."

"Right!"

"Officer Murphy, did you see the size of that big ass glass?"

"Yes, and I'm glad no one was hurt."

"Well, we were safe on both sides sir. We kept our distance as we all watched it fall."

"But once again, why this building?"

"I needed someone who was just as tired of this woman as I was, so I nominated the person who made her ass crazy."

"Who?"

"Her husband Donald, let him give his soon-to-be ex-wife my message!"

"And the message was, wait a minute I have it in the security officer's statement, tell Donald to tell his ex-wife, Ivana, that I didn't appreciate her not keeping her word!"

"And you think Donald Trump is going to tell his ex-wife, Ivana, that?"

"I can assure you that Donald is looking for a reason to call Ivana a bitch, can you imagine how that's going to sound coming off his tongue?"

"Well, maybe you have to be a divorcee or a person who's going through a bad separation, to understand the anger between a couple and how vicious it can get. "Are you divorced?"

"Hell no, I love my wife. I've been with my wife since the ninth grade."

As Officer Murphy was behind the wheel, I looked over at Officer Russo who was slightly leaning toward the armrest, as if he was having trouble breathing or having a heart attack. My heart began to beat faster hoping this policeman was okay and not having a heart attack.

The whole police car became completely quiet as the officer looked slumped in the seat leaning on the armrest. Then I ask, "Officer Murphy, is Officer Russo, okay?"

"Yeah, he's okay, he's going through a vicious

separation as we speak, he's just being an asshole right now!"

"What?"

"Yo, stop laughing asshole. Yo, Russo! We're right in fuckin front of Trump Towers and the security guards are looking at you, stop laughing!"

Now laughing in the back seat unable to stop, Officer Murphy rolled up the driver-side window so none of the guards could hear us laughing. Then out of nowhere I heard Officer Russo shout out, "Bitchhh, look what just happened because of you!" Now all three of us were laughing uncontrollably in the police car. Finally, Officer Murphy put the car in drive and pulled off from in front of Trump Towers. We were only doing three miles per hour with the lights on while we all tried to regain our composure.

Even Officer Murphy got in on it shouting out, "That's why I'm leaving you!" The laughter started up all over again. Officer Murphy continued, "You came all the way down from Atlantic City with four bricks to leave a message?"

"Yelp!"

"You're my Superhero!"

"What! What do you mean?"

"Donald Trump may have buildings in New York,

Florida, and in AC, but you're the *godfather* of AC."

"How much damage do you think was done, Officer Murphy?"

"The guard put down roughly that the window is about $25 to $30,000!"

"Are they going to put that on my Discover Card, Officer Russo? And discover there isn't shit on it."

We started laughing as we entered the precinct. As the night went on, shipped from the precinct to downtown to central booking on a blue bus to One Hundred Centre Street in Lower Manhattan, as everyone exited off the bus in handcuffs one guard stopped me and said, "So, Officer Russo said that you're the *godfather* of Atlantic City!"

Smiling at the police officer and keeping it moving, this was not the time for me to be humble, nice, or soft. Sitting in a pod with about twenty-five other men, handcuffed to a man who had a pack of cigarettes but no matches. Fortunately, I had matches, and I knew how to split them in half to make two from them, handcuffed to a bench with the cigarette man, some fool sat down across from me began to shout, "CO, CO, CO?" One of the officers walked up to him and said, "We're not CO's, We're New York City police officers and if you continue to call us CO's, I will beat your ass right here and now!"

The officer walked away from the man, stopped in front of me and said, "Officer Russo said to look out for you and that you're the *godfather* of Atlantic City!"

"Oh yeah?"

"Oh yeah, and if Russo says something, you better believe it."

Smiling the *godfather* said, "Officer Russo is a good dude! Can you loosen up the cuffs just a little for me, Officer?"

"Absolutely!"

He loosened up the cuffs. "How about that, loose enough?"

"Yes, sir!"

He walked away smiling, everyone in the pod wanted to know who this *godfather* was. People on the other side were trying to get a glimpse of me, remaining quiet, one of the detainees began to ask me questions. "So why do they call you the *godfather* of AC?"

"Because I had a problem with Donald Trump's bitch, I had to leave him a message."

"Do you mean Donald Trump, like in Atlantic City?"

"There's only one Donald Trump!"

"My man! That's what I'm talking about."

"So, are you from Atlantic City? Is that where you were born?"

"No, I was born just over the bridge in Brooklyn."

"What!"

"I was born in Brooklyn in Kings County Hospital."

"What, me too, that's where I was born. I lived on Herkimer St."

"Okay, but I was born way before your time."

"So, you went from Brooklyn to Atlantic City?

"Yelp, I stopped and lived in Chester, Pennsylvania, and North Philadelphia for a minute, but I was in Atlantic City before the casinos were there."

"See that's what I'm talking about, a motherfucka real forefather, you're a true' G."

"What?"

"You're like the second wave of Atlantic City."

"Oh yeah?"

"Hell yeah!"

"Well, who was the first wave?"

"That's when Al Capone came to Atlantic City and was walking on the Boardwalk!"

"Damn! You really went back on me."

"If you ever need to be ready for a war, we're here for you my G."

"Thank you."

"We need to exchange numbers, my G, because I got them things, I guarantee you that millionaires all listen and know that universal sound!"

"What sound is that?"

"Click, click. If you cock that steel, they damn sure will!"

"Will what?"

"Will do whatever the fuck you want them to do!"

The captives all started laughing, a lot of them began to ask me questions about their case as if they were talking to a practicing criminal lawyer. Some of them were easy to judge just by listening and saying, "You fucked up!" Taught some of the police officer's the best way to play craps, it did make my stay go by a lot quicker. My night of action was done, didn't need guns or a bunch of people behind me. Besides, my buzz was wearing off.

After looking at a bologna and cheese sandwich with four fingers and a thumbprint visible on the bread, not to mention the big ass bug that carried it away off my paper plate was very impressive. There were few hours left before going into the courtroom to see the judge and be arraigned on my charges. A police officer called out my name. Standing up and raised my hand, another police officer uncuffed me from the cigarette man. As I walked up to the window, the police officer at the window asked me, "Is this your correct name and address?"

"Yes, sir!"

"And is all this information, correct?"

"Yes, sir!"

"Why do they call you the *godfather* of Atlantic City?"

"Because, just maybe, that's who the fuck I am!" Then I smiled and said, "Can I have that orange right there, Officer?"

"My orange?"

"Yeah, your orange!"

"Here!"

"Thanks! And tell Officer Russo that you gave me your

orange."

"Crazy Russo."

"He'll thank you. I might come back down to be Russo's therapist on weekends."

Everyone started laughing, and someone shouted out, "Russo can use a therapist!" The officer gave me his orange as I was escorted out into another holding pod and was searched again. This was right before you saw the judge, and unlike the last search this one was more detailed as the officers gave you a chance this time to remove anything that you're not supposed to have.

"This is your first, last, and only warning, if you have anything in your pockets or in your possession that's not supposed to be there, take it out and put it on the floor right now! If we search you and prick our fingers on a needle or knife or any other sharp objects, you will not live to talk about it."

"Okay!"

"Take your shoes off set them on the floor and take four steps forward."

A joint was still in my sock up by my toes. It probably had toe jam, sock-lint and sweat on it but I wasn't giving that up for anyone! Before seeing the judge, they let me speak to someone who was part of the public defender's office who ask,

"Can you afford an attorney?"

"Yes, sir!"

"Do you have an attorney?"

"Yes, I do, what am I being charged with?"

"From what it looks like, they're charging you with felony burglary and possession of burglary tools!"

"Oh really?"

"Yes, sir!"

"Guess that's because I stole everyone's peace last night."

"Well, Mr. Trump's lawyers made sure that I knew that Donald Trump is really pissed at you, he wants you prosecuted to the full extent of the law."

"Really?"

"Now that's what I'm talking about, Donald sounds angry. It sounds like Donald got my message; he's just as pissed off as I was when locked up by his wife Ivana."

"He also wants you to pay for the repairs of the glass!"

"What are his lawyers saying that the glass cost?"

"The lawyers said approximately $26,000 to $40,000, and Donald wants you to pay any charges for additional security because it's going to take a few days to have that glass repaired."

"Well, that's good to know, that'll give more residents time to complain about that breeze!"

"What?"

"Please send a note to Donald Trump's lawyers for me!"

"Aren't you tired of leaving messages yet?"

"Yes, but can you write this down for me, sir?"

"Yes, go right ahead."

"Tell Donald Trump's lawyers to tell their boss, Mr. Trump, to tell his soon-to-be ex-wife Ivana, the message that's on the police report and if he doesn't tell her, tell Donald Trump's lawyers that I said fuck his window."

"So there has been litigation between your lawyer and the Trump organization?"

"Yes sir, this shit didn't just start!"

"Can you give me a number for your lawyers?"

"Yes, sir, his name is Robert B. Clark, and his office is located at 654 Central Ave., East Orange, New Jersey."

"What's his phone number?"

"His number is 201-xxx-xxxx"

"Okay!"

"When you speak to him."

"Yeah?"

"Could you please tell Mr. Clark that I'm going to fuck him up, with his fat ass the first chance I get!"

"Is there any other lawyer?"

"Yes! His name is William Bromley, out of Atlantic City, New Jersey. His office is located somewhere in the 12 or 1300 hundred blocks of Atlantic Ave. His phone 609-xxx-xxxx. When you talk to him, tell him to make an appointment for me in a few days."

"Mr. G, can I ask you a personal question?"

"Yes, sir!"

"On the bottom of this page right here, it has in very small print the *godfather* of Atlantic City! Is that you?"

"If that's what you choose to call me, cool!"

"Well, we're going to scribble that out, we don't need no

extra questions from the judge!"

"Absolutely agree. I'm sure there's been a lot of questions so far."

"Look, when we go in front of the judge, just answer the question she asks, and let me do the talking!"

"Okay!"

"You do want to go home to your family and wife today, don't you?"

"Absolutely!"

"Maybe we can talk Trump and his lawyers into taking both cases and combining the two of them." At that point it hit me, not only was felony burglary on the table, but my wife who really matter to me had to be told about all of this. "Well, I'm sure you want to see your wife."

"Going to have to ride this one out! She's going to be mad at me and she should be but as long as there's this chip on my shoulder and feelings so heavy on my heart, nothing good was going to happen in my life. Must change my ways and my way of thinking, must De-Trumpilize."

"Well, you better do something, because if you come back to New York, you're going to be here for a while."

"Promise you I'll be back up here to handle this

situation."

"I hope so!"

"Just not on that date."

"Well,' I'm only worried about today!"

"Okay, feel a lot better now. Haven't felt this good in years, feeling liberated, maybe I'll buy an instant camera and go back up there just to get a picture with that big ass window."

"If you go back up there right now, they will lock you up on sight and take you straight to the island."

"Nah, no fight left in me, had enough excitement for the night."

"So, if I can get Trump's lawyers to combine the suit with the burglary, maybe we can get the charges reduced."

"Cool. If they don't want to make a deal, tell Donald's lawyers that I said, forgot her hair!"

"Say what?"

"Read my lips! Tell Trump's lawyers I said, FORGOT HER HAIR!"

He wrote my message down on his pad and walked away shaking his head from left to right. Finally, it was my turn to see the judge, her name was Judge Judy. Just before we went through the doors, he stopped me in my tracks and asked me, "Do you want to go home to your family and wife today?"

"Yes, I do!"

"Then do yourself a big favor, half of this shit on this paper and in your statements, I'm afraid to even mention them to the judge!"

"Yeah, but it is what it is!"

"Well, I hope the judge is in a good mood and she doesn't feel bad herself."

"You don't think going to Rikers Islands for years, the possibility of someone shooting me, hadn't crossed my mind before boarding that bus with them four bricks?"

"Yes, but your fight is in Atlantic City."

"Maybe it was at one time, but it's in both of our hometowns tonight!"

"What?"

"He was born in Queens, and I was born in Brooklyn, so we're on even grounds."

"Well! It is what it is."

"I know that."

"You know what?"

"It is what it is!"

"Well!"

"Why do you think I bought four bricks with me?"

"I don't know, why?"

"Because I needed to deliver a message!"

"Well, I hope the judge doesn't want to send you a message!"

"If they do, I came mentally prepared for that."

"Like what?"

"I knew I was going to jail when I got on the bus in Atlantic City."

"And you still came to New York?"

"Yes! But I did take extra precautions!"

"How?"

"I needed to make sure my message was delivered, that means if it didn't break the first time, there were three more bricks to try, try again then try harder, and just do it!"

"Now I can see there's more to this story than what catches the eye."

"Good! You have no idea."

"I couldn't get in contact with Mr. Robert B. Clark!"

"Were you able to leave him a message?"

"Yes, I did."

"Great!"

"But it wasn't the message, that you were going to hurt him!"

"Did you say my name on the message?"

"Yes!"

"Good, because he knows what that means!"

"I did talk to William Bromley!"

"Oh yeah?"

"Yes, very nice man, he said to call his office when you get home, and that he'll look forward to seeing you in a few days."

"Great!"

"So please, *please* don't make my morning long, please!"

"Okay!"

"Let me do all the talking, please?"

"You got it. I really miss my wife!"

"Okay! Let's try to get you outta here."

As we walked into the courtroom with me in handcuffs, needing to cooperate, homesick, as the judge read off my charges, all my mind heard was the Charlie Brown schoolteacher's voice, "Qaumm qaumm, qaumm, qaumm." Think about my wife, things taken for granted, realizing how missing my wife hurt, hearing the judge and the public defender talking in the background, as crazy as it sounded there were small things being realized about myself. Such as what was important in my life. A lot of my everyday activities every night were truly blessings. My greatest blessing being my wife. Not only do I love her, but I'm also still in love with this woman and must do better. She had told me about my potty mouth since I'd been driving a cab at night, causing me to learn to stop and substitute other words for the bad ones.

Learn from this, it was selfish to put this Trump fight first! I miss my friend, her smile, her two big dimples, her scent, her body heat, her hair touching my face, the two of us heating up our feet together, locking my legs around hers, her laugh, her touch, kissing her on the back of her neck softly while her head is lying on my right arm, pulling her body close to mine with my left arm until we're locked in a perfect S position as one, and whispering in her ear, "I love you."

Back in the courtroom, started hearing numbers like, 2 to 5 years, $24 to $37,000 and maybe some type of community service on Ninety-Fifth or Ninety-Eighth in the subways or Central Park for thirty days. Then realizing, *Wow, they're talking about me!* Love New York and would clean it up for free, but this had become personal. Before cleaning up any subways or parks in New York City because of Trump, why not just stay out of New York and be an outlaw, fuck it! I felt myself getting pissed all over again, waiting for the judge to say just three words, "You may leave!"

The public defender looked at me and asked, "Do you understand?" Looking at him and the judge I replied said with a clear, strong voice, "Yes, Judge!" Really didn't hear a word that was said by the judge, tiered and missing my wife, the judge could have said Jack be nimbo, Jack be quick, Jack jump over the candlestick, qaumm qaumm, qaumm qaumm!" So, I replied by saying "Yes, Judge!"

"Sir?"

"Yes, Judge?"

"Do you understand what I just said?"

"Yes, Judge!"

"Okay, I'm releasing you today, and your counsel will have your court date and all of your paperwork, sir!"

"Yes, ma'am!"

"And your counsel had the chance to talk to an attorney from Atlantic City also, so please do follow up with that meeting when you get back to Atlantic City!"

"Yes, Judge!"

"Do you have any questions, sir?"

"No, Judge."

"Thank you, and you may leave, have a good day sir!"

"Trust me Judge, I will have a great day thank you."

My public defender walked behind me. "Are you going to make this court date?"

"I doubt it, but if Donald's lawyers call you, tell them that security guard Rick has my card and number."

"You know if you don't make that court date, they're going to issue a bench warrant on you!"

"Oh, okay! Can I call you to defend me?"

"Forgot her hair!" We both started laughing, although no one could find my Walkman with that hot tape in it, they said that I had to go all the way to Queens, New York for it. That was too close to Rikers Island for me. Free at last, free at last, was ringing in my head while walking out of One Hundred Centre Street in Lower Manhattan. Really wanted to see that window.

The fresh air and the steam coming from the manhole covers never smelt so damn good! Only one other smell was wanted, my wife's! Walked toward Chinatown, stopped and called my wife. After leaving her a nice message, it would soon be time to do a lot of explaining. So, singing Teddy Riley's song "Jam, Jam, Jam" the realization hit me that the joint up by my toes was still there. After stopping, taking my shoe and sock off, retrieved my joint of sinsemilla, continued to sing "Jam" while picking the lint off the joint. "Jam Jam, Jam" continued to play, lit up my joint, while walking to catch the subway.

The sun was coming up, it reminded me of coming up to New York City just to hang out with my girl. Now my wifey, we had a lot of fun up here hanging out at Studio 54 with a group called unlimited Touch, D-Train, or going to the Garage on King Street, or Bentleys on Fortieth, or Roxy's.   The fresh air never smelt better as the vapors came from the subway. Soon started laughing to myself thinking about that big ass window! After all that glass fell, we were all eye level, and it seemed to get quiet after the last piece of glass dropped.

It was *so* quiet for about ten seconds as we all just stared at each other, looking at them as they all looked at me. Then "Getthimm!" suddenly burst out laughing. The people on the train must have thought me crazy because of all the uncontrolled laughing. Even Ivana Trump, was probably happy to see someone stand up to her soon-to-be ex-husband Donald. Hey, maybe she was glad that someone broke that big ass window. After all she was a victim of Donald as me. Feeling bad for her, although she was no longer staying at the Towers, imagine Ivana Trump with her accent saying, "I'm glad he broke that big ass glass Donald, let your homewrecking bitch fix it. That's what you get for dumping me!" Not making that court date because of other conflicts, meant not being able visit NYC for a while. Maybe go to Queens, New York, get my Walkman, tape, some White Castles and Nathan's French fries. Nope! Needed to get my ass on the bus and back to Atlantic City. So, back to Port Authority bus station with my round- trip ticket to AC.

Back to AC, Face the Wife, More Lawyers!

After a long hot one-hour shower and some much-needed rest, along with a great dinner, this night was different. Talking about sexual healing, passion, heat, more passion, less healing, more heat, less passion. Wow! We may have made a baby. Life was good again.

Couldn't stop thinking about that window, still want to see that big empty space again while sober. After some time went by, finally saw William Bromley even if it was just for some advice. Pretty much just needed a friend.

However, the lawyer in North Jersey Robert B. Clark, was a different story. He was made an offer that could have and should have refused but chose to accept it. Taking my money, meant another visit. If things didn't work out like before, jail could again be in my future. The plan was to *make my appointment with Bromley first, then I'll go to see Clark.* Some time had passed and my court date in New York had come and gone.

After giving Mr. Bromley the court information from New York and asking him to investigate, get some answers, or at least have a response from the courts before the time of my next scheduled appointment with him. He said he would see what he could do. Having an active warrant made me a fugitive/outlaw in the state of New York. Now, just a straight-out rebel for downright refusing to clean up any subways or parks because of Donald. This was my misplaced way of proving myself to Mr. Trump, by not being afraid of his organization, to earn his respect, validating his team's prior hiring decision.

The longer it took for them to repair that big ass window, the more people had time to look at that big ass space and complain. It would be great to have his best friend Regis

Philbin, who was living there at the time, to call Donald Trump directly on his hotline and say, "It's a mothafuckin' breeze coming up the stairs and elevator shafts, what is going on, Donald?" It would also been nice to have anyone who opposed the marriage between Donald and Ivana to point a finger saying, "We told you Donald, not to marry her."

Needing to talk with Mr. Bromley ASAP, maybe he could convince me to turn off this switch that still had me negatively focused on the Trump incident. Instead, Clark was next on my list. It had been several weeks since my New York trip, *Today was the day to talk with Bromley and to be honest, it wasn't even about the big ass window anymore.* His feedback was going to make or break me. The truth would be acceptable but miss me with the bullshit.

Mr. Bromley had been paid to make a phone call, nothing more and nothing less, just a phone call. Sitting in Bromley's waiting room, he had a small office with awards all over his walls, the pictures showed much respect from just about every lawyer on the East Coast. Waiting patiently, finally it was my turn, "Hello, Mr. Bromley!"

"Well, we finally get a chance to meet."

"What a pleasure sir."

"Okay, I had a chance to talk to the courts in New York City, my advice to you is if you go there don't get caught.

Because if you do, you're going to be there for a while, so just stay out of New York for now."

"Thanks, but what I need to talk to you about is this piece-of-shit lawyer that's been representing me."

"What has he been doing for you?"

"Well right now, he hasn't been doing anything including communicating with me."

"How long has it been since you've talked to him?"

"It's been a while since we've talked, and now I get the message from the secretary that he's in court and to be honest, the last time we talked it wasn't much of a conversation."

"What do you mean, it wasn't much of a conversation?"

"The last time we saw each other in person, he wasn't expecting the visit."

"What do you mean expecting the visit?"

"The last time I spoke to Mr. Clark, I told him my name was Tyrone Green and I was on a New Jersey Transit bus, when it was hit by a limo. My grandmother asked me to call, and his secretary kindly made an appointment for me."

"And what happened at that appointment?"

"I went up there with a friend Curtis, who stayed in the car. When Clark's secretary went into his office, I looked all over, even on the floor until I spotted my files. When he came back in the waiting room with his receptionist, he turned pale and began to stutter. Looking at her he said, "That's not Tyrone Green, his name is Steve, and I wasn't at all expecting him, but rather someone else!"

My response was, "Well, while am I here, I need to pick up my file!"

"Well, you should have called, because your files are not ready yet."

"Well, I think they are ready now, as a matter of fact, they're so ready there in my briefcase already!"

"If you walk out of this office with that file, I'm going to call the police and say that you assaulted me and my secretary."

"If you touch that phone before I touched that doorknob, your secretary is going to be explaining what the fuck happened to your fat ass." After closing the door and counted to three, reopened the door, they were still standing there in disbelief, closed the door, headed down the back steps and jumped in the car.

Mr. Bromley then asked, "Did the police ever come to your house?"

"No, they never came or called me."

"Wow!"

"Don't think they called the police. It was probably just a scare tactic. The bad part for him is that fear shit doesn't work on me. Because Almighty God is my only fear!

"As we talked before, I told you that your case is too

contaminated from other lawyers, that's why I can't take it."

"Well, can you make a phone call for me?"

"Who do you want me to call?"

"Call up my last lawyer, Robert B. Clark, and ask him if he is willing to reinstate that case!"

"What case?"

"Me vs. Trump, after getting my files back, they clearly showed that the case had been dismissed."

"Why was it dismissed?"

"Because Clark failed to attend an early conference settlement!"

"Really?"

"Yes, sir!"

"Okay, call me Bill!"

"Okay Bill, Clark told me that it was a mistake and he's going to send in the necessary documents to have it reinstated."

"That's not a conference that many lawyers would miss. Look, here's what I'll do for you. I'll call Mr. Clark and see exactly where this case is at, but I need you to know that I am not taking your case! I don't represent you."

"Got it!"

"I'm going to make the call because I'm curious why he didn't reinstate the case immediately or make the hearing."

"You're either going to tell me that I'm crazy or Trump lawyers got to my ex-lawyer Robert B. Clark, who's a piece of shit."

"Is there any other thing you need to tell me before I call Clark?"

"Yes, Bill. During my first meeting Robert Clark, it was explained to him that trust in a lawyer was needed most. It didn't matter if it ended up being a win, lose, or draw, as long as my lawyer heard me, was honest and still had my trust. He could see how desperate my need was for a lawyer, with cash in front of him, clearly this was my wit's end. Clark needed to make a conscious decision before he took my money and case! It was important to me that Clark knew not to fuck me over. He needed to look me in my eyes before he took my cash to let me know that he understood that it was all becoming too much for me to handle and consuming my life. And there was one condition for him that was personal."

Bill asked, "What was the condition?"

"Just that he needed to think long and hard before he took my money. Because if he takes my money and then fucks me over intentionally, this situation will become his worst nightmare!"

"Well, right now he's still alive and practicing law."

"Yeah, we both caught a big break two months ago."

"What do you mean? What happened two months ago that I need to know about?"

"To make good on my promise to Mr. Clark, my friend Curtis rode with me just for support, up to Central Avenue in

East Orange New Jersey. Curtis wasn't going to do anything, wasn't even packing a piece."

"Were there any weapons with you?"

"Excuse me?"

"Were you packing a piece?"

"Maybe, it's easier to buy a piece off the streets than it was to find a lawyer who doesn't want to work for the Trumps. Just in case in the car, there may have been two guns, a big ass baseball bat, a knife, and my timberland boots were on. All of this just in case a decision was made to fuck him up!"

"What happened next?"

"My plan was to go up to Clark's office and just flatten a tire on his car. Then when he came downstairs to look at or change the flat, let him have it. He always stayed in his office to at least at 5:00 p.m."

"Okay! Go ahead!"

"When he gets off work, it's just beginning to get dark outside, and it would be a wrap for Clark!"

"What do you mean, a wrap?"

"It's a wrap, that's all she wrote, the fat lady has sung her last song, he bought this on himself. To be totally honest, I really don't know what would have happened, if I'd didn't have that talk."

"What happened next?"

"After I hit his tire, time needed it to pass for it to get darker. So, we drove over to New York City to kill some time.

As Curtis talked with me as we were stuck in traffic on the New Jersey turnpike. A helicopter had crashed into the Hudson River or some other river, fortunately that was the best thing that ever happened for me."

"Why is that?"

"Because it gave my friend a chance to be a real friend and have a heart-to-heart talk with me."

The conversation started out by Curt saying, "You do know that once you cross that line, there's no turning back or taking back."

"Yeah, I know."

"That's it!"

"Are you sure you want to serve this asshole today?"

"If I don't, it'll be swept under the carpet as just another bad attorney."

"Yeah, but he's not the first bad attorney, and he's not going to be the last either!"

"That shit will stay on my mind."

"But that's going to happen regardless of whether you do anything to this piece of shit or not."

"At least this piece of shit lawyer won't fuck someone else over."

"So, you're going to sacrifice your life, freedom, and time today for this piece of shit?"

"It will only be a sacrifice if I get caught!" We both began to laugh, but he was right.

"And besides, your fight is between you and the Trump organization."

Asking myself, was it worth giving up everything including my family over my feelings and emotions about Clark? Was being anger really a solid justification? After repeatedly questioning myself, knowing that this wasn't my life just what it's turning into. Could last night have been the last time seeing or holding my wife and kid? To make a long story short, the right decision was made not to give up the most important thing in my life, which is my wife and family.

"You're fortunate to have a friend like Curtis."

"Yeah, a fake friend would've told me what I wanted to hear; Curtis told me what I needed to hear."

"So, what happened next?"

"After we got to New York, ate some White Castles, this bitch ass lawyer Clark was no longer of any important to me. On the way back to Atlantic City, we went back to see if his car was still there. Not planning to stop or anything but still wanting him to see me. As we pulled up in the back parking lot, we realized that his car was still there, then Curtis shout, "Don't stop, don't stop, keep driven there are two undercover cops staring at us over on the right, keep going!" We kept going but there was a good chance that they got my tagged number."

Bill said, "As long as you didn't stop and get out, you're okay, unless they had cameras around."

"Well! It is what it is. Maybe it will cost me the price of a tire or two."

"I need you to stay out of New York, North Jersey, and most of all, trouble!"

"Okay!"

"I'll get back to you as soon as I hear something back from Clark."

"I'll be waiting and thank you Bill."

Walking out of his office, for some strange reason it felt lighter, like a weight had been lifted. It wasn't about that big ass window, just needed one person of sound mind to trust and restore my faith in humanity.

Comfortable now and believed in Mr. Bromley things were getting better. Before speaking with Bill, my faith in the judicial system was almost completely lost. My belief in mainly the lawyers or any people who wanted to work for Donald Trump had been destroyed. Several months went by without hearing from Mr. Bromley, but on one morning while getting off work, a phone call from Mr. Bromley's office requested to come to his office as soon as possible. After making an appointment for four that afternoon my curiosity about why he needed to see me on such short notice was very high. Arriving at his office his secretary was expecting me. When Mr. Bromley came out of his office, he didn't shake my hand. Instead, he looked at me without saying a word and pointed for me to come into his inner office. He seemed like he had a real bad attitude. My heart was beating hard, why, I don't know. Bill said, "Have a seat, Mr. G!"

Final Consequences!

He walked around his office, hitting his fist into his other hand. It seemed like the same anger that had been in me, the same anger that caused me to punch that piece shit in his eye way back during the fight at the Castle, the same anger that caused me to throw those bricks through that big ass glass, the same anger that got me locked up at Ivana's office. Why was he's so pissed was the question?

Bill then said, "I had a chance to talk to Mr. Clark and his secretary on numerous occasions over the past several months. Mr. Clark promised me some documents. It was just as simple matter of emailing them to me. Now he's not returning my calls, and his secretary is giving me excuses on why he's not in the office."

"Really?"

"How old are you, Mr. G?"

"Thirty years old, Bill."

"Well, I've been practicing law longer than you've been on this planet and I've never sued another lawyer, but this piece of shit Clark is going to hear from me. If you had killed Clark, I would've defended you!"

"What?"

"No! I don't want you to do nothing!"

"Okay, good!"

"I'm going to file an ethics complaint against him."

"What's that?"

"Never mind. I'm going to have him disbarred from practicing law in this or any other state. I cannot believe his ignorance. I've never seen such neglect since I've been practicing law and never ran across a stupid ass lawyer like this."

"So, it's not me, I'm not crazy, right?"

"No my friend, you're not crazy at all, but Clark is."

Jumping out of my chair with enjoy, "Well look I'm ready to go to war, I can get almost any type of weapon on the planet and all the people we need to go get Clark."

Bill said, "I'm going to take this case on one condition, and one condition only. You have to agree to it today or leave my office with no questions asked!"

Having no idea what he wanted me to agree to, my firstborn, my house, cash, "Okay. What do you want me to agree to, Bill"?

"Sit down!" Bill put his hand on my right shoulder. "You have to agree from this day forward that you're going to take your life back, focus on your family, wife, home and move forward with your life. I can't do anything about Trump, but let me handle this Clark person, okay?"

Being tough and still looking for fault in this man, for Bill to take the time to make one call that may have made a big difference in my life, big ass tears were building in my eyes. Nothing to lose, tired, missing my family, my emotions were getting the best of me. Not even sure my wife, family, and home, were still there to go back to because I'd given up my entire life to fight the Trumps. My wife had been holding it all down for me. Tired of looking for lawyers, having given my message to Donald Trump and his organization when I went up there with them four bricks, not trying to be a Gangsta, that's not me, it was time to get my life back. Those big ass tears started rolling down my face, "Deal!"

"No more calls to Clark!"

"Deal!"

"No more late-night visits to New York City!"

"Deal!"

"No more riding up to East Orange, New Jersey, to see Mr. Clark!"

"Deal!"

"Last, but not least, no more bricks near any of Trump's properties or anyone else's property!"

"Deal, deal, deal, and thank you, Bill!"

"Now as far as the window, Trump's lawyers are saying that it's going to cost about $45,000 to $60,000 for that window."

"Wow! I heard that Donald was pissed at me too."

"I would think so! And that's a lot of money to pay back, the lawyer said that the window glass was so big that they had to build a new frame with smaller pieces of glass in it temporally, until they had a new glass that size."

"Oh, okay!"

"So, my suggestion to you is to stay out of New York City! No, if, ands, or buts just stay out of New York!"

"Yes, sir!"

"I'll get back to you soon!"

Walking out onto Atlantic Avenue in AC, thinking about how best to take back my life, the courts still had a lot to say about how that was going to go. On June 29, 1992, the court assigned me to an alternative sentencing program in New York City by Judge Harris Kluger for violating PL 240.20. The program required me to do community service on Ninety-Seventh Street in Manhattan, New York. Failure to complete the program would result in me doing fifteen days at Rikers Island.

On June 30, 1992, I violated my community service. The last thing on my mind was that big ass glass or Donald's money. Go to New York to help clean up on my own would make my heart smile, doing because of Donald would not. It was time for me to take on a serious mission. Having no idea where to start taking my life, the need for coming up with a lot of money for some good lawyers was clear. If not, my label would be felon for the rest of my life.

Having to stay out of New York City didn't sit well with me at all. In December of 1992, my wife gave birth to our son, that was my starting point. Knowing he needed me, my other son needed me, I needed them, and we all needed my wife, this became my motivation.

It had been months since hearing from Mr. Bromley, being in good hands with him, allowed me to stay focused on what really mattered, my second chance to live life with my wife, family, kids, dog, and friends.

On this morning, there was a missed call on my phone. It was from Mr. Bromley's office. His message urgently wanted me to get in contact with his office. Although exhausted from working the night before, not having the nicest attitude, called him back right anyway. His secretary put me on a brief hold and then connected me to Mr. Bromley, "Mr. G, how are you doing, my friend?"

"I'm well Bill, just working hard!"

"How is the wife and kids, they good?"

"Yes, thank you!"

"Have you been staying out of trouble?"

"Trouble, as in?"

"Trouble, as in New York City or any other situation we talked about?"

"Absolutely not! Can't allow myself to go backwards, mainly back to thinking about that situation, or that old thinking and attitude of mine. Knowing better, you do better!"

"That's good news. Now I have some great news!"

"Well, I can always use that!"

"We won a judgment against Clark!"

"What! Forgot her hair!"

"What?"

"Don't pay that no mind, just trying to stop cursing."

"I'm proud of you for taking your life back."

"Thank you for making that call, taking that case, and giving me a chance to get my life back on track."

"The only problem is that I'm not going to be able to pursue the collection part."

"Why?"

"You're going to have to get another lawyer to go after

the settlement because I'm not that healthy right now."

"Don't worry Bill, I can get a few guys to go with me and get our money."

"NOOO! I need you to continue doing exactly what you're doing, take care of your family and live your life."

"Promise Bill, I'm staying focused."

"Okay good!"

"If not one dime comes from that case, it wouldn't matter to me."

"Why do you say that?"

"You gave me something that money can't buy."

"Like what?"

"You gave me back my life, my dignity, my trust, my time, all of that's priceless!"

"Enjoy your life my friend, enjoy it."

"Will do."

"Look! They gave us a judgment of $133,398.10 plus interest until you collect!"

"Wow!"

"But I need you to stay out of trouble and New York City!"

"Well, I'm staying out of trouble, but New York may be a different story."

"You are aware that if you get caught in New York City, you're going to be there for a while my friend."

"Promise Bill, I'm going to handle that New York situation like you, very cool, calm, and collected, and very soon, without going to jail."

"If you should receive something from the Ethics Committee, contact me here at my firm ASAP."

"Will do."

"Are you still on that crazy shift?"

"Yes, and from what I hear I don't have the nicest attitude." Bill burst out laughing and coughing.

"Are you alright?"

"Yes, I have your file in front of me, and I'm looking at the police report from New York City. You have chutzpah!"

"What's that?"

"Big balls."

"Yeah, I just had a baby, remember." We both burst out into laughter.

"How did you hold that brick again?"

"Do you remember that Bugs Bunny powerhouse song? How Bugs would wind things up using song?"

The laughing started again and lasted for a full minute this time. After hanging up the phone, did something that should have been done before going to New York or East Orange, New Jersey, closed my eyes and said a heartfelt prayer. Asked the

Lord to keep me humble, never ever let me get so overwhelmed or anger to take matters into my own hands. No matter how bad a person treats me, learn to hit back with kindness like Bill. Don't go down to their level, don't lose complete control of my anger. That was a promise to me and family.

On February 2, 1993, the judgment was reduced. It didn't matter, still have my wife, my oldest son, my new baby boy, was blessing enough for me.

In August of 1994, Mr. Bromley passed away. The best way for me to honor Bill's life was to live my life to the fullest. Because of his generosity, integrity, and empathy it was possible to put the past in the past—well, almost. Still had to take care of that little situation in New York.

On October 6, 1994, at 2:00 p.m., I was invited to a Supreme Court of New Jersey, Ethics Committee hearing by Andrew A. McDonald, Esq. and Charles B. Clancy III, Esq. Mr. Andrew was my contact person for this matter. When we first started talking about Clark, Mr. Andrew was told that if the committee didn't discipline Clark, it would still be handled. He reminded me how important it was to keep a level head during the hearing.

Instead of retaining yet another lawyer to explain what is so obvious, a letter was sent to the Ethics Committee, advising them that my friend/lawyer Mr. Bromley was no longer with us, and there's no way to find a lawyer who had the chutzpah, compassion, integrity, empathy, heart, common sense as far as right and wrong, and respect for his oath to the bar that Mr. Bromley had on such short notice. Therefore, my plan is to attend the hearing alone with all my documentation, feeling sure that Mr. Bromley will be there in my heart. Just because Mr. Bromley was no longer with us, no one should take my kindness for weakness or that my side was backing down. Keeping a level head would be easy because the truth was consistent and on my side.

If you throw the truth in the air, when it comes back down, hits the hard surface of reality, it will break into hundreds of pieces. Once back together it's still the truth. Just in case being prepared for Clark's bullshit feelings, was necessary. On the day of the meeting, it was only me and my documentations. Everything organized just in case it was needed.

The meeting was with the DEC at that time. Communicating with Mr. Peter S. Valentine had allowed me to have all my documents listed as Exhibits 1, 2, 3, and so forth. As we sat across from each other, Clark refused to make eye contact. Mr. Valentine began to rip into Clark's ass like there was no tomorrow, for leaving the first DEC meeting, he went on saying, "The DEC found respondent Clark guilty of violating RPC 1.1 (A), RPC 1.3, and RPC 8.1." Clark shouted out, "My mother was ill in another state!"

"What about these letters that you've ignored from the lawyers?" Clark shouted out, "I was unfamiliar with the procedures in Atlantic County, and I missed the first meeting because my mother who lives in Michigan had suffered two strokes the week of the hearing and was critically, perhaps terminally ill."

"Clark is guilty of unethical conduct, and definitely he exhibited gross neglect and a lack of diligence."

Clark began talking and again explaining about how his mother was in Michigan and very ill at that time so he couldn't focus on my situation. Mr. Clark couldn't look me in the eyes. Badly wanting to reach over the table and slap the shit out of him, my level head had me looked at Peter and pointed to a paragraph that clearly showed that it's been over a year.

Peter began to rip Clark a new asshole again, seeing that anger in Peter allowed me to keep my composure. Leaping across the table with an open hand drawn way back and just slap the spit out of his mouth, would have really felt good.

Representing myself, and in affect Bill Bromley, any kind of ignorance from me would have made all of Mr. Bromley's hard work in vain. That wasn't Mr. Bromley's style, he was cool, calm, and collected. Getting the opportunity to talk to Peter one on one after the hearing, he felt there was a lot more to this situation than his mother being sick. For some strange reason, I felt so much better just to have been heard. Peter said, "Hello, Mr. G, I just want to thank you for taking the time out of your day to make it to this hearing."

"Thank you for listening to my grievance."

"Most of the lawyers take their oath to the bar very seriously, but there's always that one."

"What happens from here?"

"The committee will go over all the information that was provided and decide what type of punishment should be imposed."

"Honestly Mr. Valentine, just seeing that the complaint wasn't being thrown under the carpet, made me feel better."

"If it wasn't for your persistence, it probably would've been thrown or swept under the carpet."

"Well, keep me posted."

"I will, but I have a few gentlemen I would like for you to meet."

As we walk across the room, he began introducing me to other members of the committee. It was cool to see how much support the committee supported my position. One of the panelists asked me, "Did you really leave a message at Trump Towers?"

"Really wasn't expecting that question, but I did have an odd way of communicating with the Trumps. Yes, I did."

Everyone started laughing, wasn't sure how much information Mr. Bromley had provided to the committee, but still hoped they do the right thing. My day was over, it was time to get some rest before work. Several months later, one morning at about 9:00 a.m. my house phone rang with a North Jersey number on it. "Hello! Can I help you?"

"Is this Mr. G?"

"Yes, it is. What can I do for you?"

"Do you want to see the tape?"

"What tape and who are you again?"

"I am a lawyer out of North Jersey, and I represent a lady who was hurt at Trump Castle during a fight on the casino floor."

"Was she a little old white lady who was at the blackjack table?"

"Yes, that's her!"

"I remember that lady well and often wonder what happened to her."

"Well, we have the tape of the fight, do you want to see

it?"

"Yes, I do. It's been several years since that day on the crap table."

"Well, we would like to set it up so we can ask you a few questions also."

"When were you thinking of meeting up?"

"Maybe Thursday?

"I can make that time available in my schedule."

"We need to be able to look at the tape on a VCR!"

"I have a few VCRs, one in my kitchen that we can use."

"Well, that will work. We also have a few documents we want you to look over!"

"Sure, you can use the kitchen table for your paperwork, you'll be comfortable."

"That's great!"

"Now, when were you thinking about coming down this way?"

"I would like to see you on Thursday how does 10:00 a.m. sound?"

"That's fine! Your law firm is in North Jersey, correct?"

"Correct!"

"I would like for your firm to look into a situation in New York City for me."

"Is it criminal, traffic court, or municipal court?"

"It's criminal!"

"Well, we're licensed to practice law in New York also, and I'm sure that we can help you with your situation."

"That's great. Looking forward to seeing you, are you coming by yourself?"

"No, I will be accompanied by a senior colleague."

"Great, see you then."

After this call, began feeling optimistic again about having this New York bullshit behind me. It would be nice to go back to New York freely without looking over my shoulder or worried about the police sending me to jail, still missing my hometown. It didn't take long for three days to go by.

On the morning of the meeting, it was only my son and I at home. Really looking forward to some answers for my New York situation. Since they wanted something from me, it's only right that they bring something to the table. Still tired from working the night before my attitude wasn't that great. Getting access to the tape would be great.

Starting to feel sad as time grew closer thinking about the tape that got my ass whipped by several security guards in Ivana Trump's office, locked up for the first time in my life, lost a good job, had to deal with a piece-of-shit lawyer, and got shitted on by Ivana Trump, a woman I trusted. My phone rang and the lawyer said, "Hello, this is the lawyer who spoke with you!"

"Yes sir, where are you guys at now?"

"We're by the Wawa on Leeds Avenue and Main Street."

"That's down the street from my house, here are the instructions to get to my home!"

"Would you like a cup of coffee this morning?"

"Yes, thank you and I'll see you soon."

Setting my son up in his room with the Power Ranger movie so we wouldn't be interrupted just before hearing the doorbell rang. Opened the door, welcomed both gentlemen into my home, led the way to my kitchen so they could set themselves up and we could get right down to business. As we made ourselves comfortable at the booth table in my kitchen, the younger gentleman asked me, "Could I use the restroom?"

"Sure!" and directed him, "Second door on the right!" The younger gentlemen went to the bathroom, the older man introduce himself to me as Lou. We sat in the kitchen as Lou briefly explained what we were going to talk about as we viewed the tape. Although this lawyer was an older lawyer, he was classy, a clean dresser, and very smooth. The other lawyer came out of the bathroom, talking about how it was laid out.

The younger lawyer returned and said, "Your bathroom looks like something you would see in a hotel suite, I never saw a home that had a heart-shaped Jacuzzi in it!"

"Yeah, that's because I married the love of my life!"

"And the whole wall has a full sheet of mirror on it."

Stepping out of the booth so the younger lawyer could slide in and said, "You even have your initial on the wall made from tile! I like your bathroom!"

"Okay. Thanks! Can we get down to business now?"

"Yes, sir. Now before we look at the video, I need to ask you a few questions!"

"Absolutely! But first and foremost, please give that little lady my regards and a hug for me."

"Okay, I will."

"After seeing her take a punch like a champ, wondered many nights what happened to her."

"Well, that's why we're here, to make sure she's okay."

"That's good to hear, okay, let's go!"

"Question number one, what is your name? Number two, what kind of day was it?" Questions umber 3, 4, 5, 6, 7, 8, 9, etc. followed.

Finally, he handed me the tape to put in the VCR. It seemed like a long walk to the VCR machine, which was only five feet from the table, but I felt a tear in my eye trying to build up anyway. Although my back was turned to the lawyers, did everything in my power not to drop this fucking tear DROP, and definitely not a in front of them. Reaching the machine, a tear fell from my eye. Hadn't hit the play button yet, but with all these emotions going through me, another teardrop fell from my other eye, what the fuck. This was the tape that didn't exist, got me beat up and handcuffed just for asking to see it, what was going to be seen besides me getting my ass whipped?

With both lawyers looking at me from the back, before hitting the play button, remembering my mama, useing both my hands to cover my face. With both eyes, said a prayer asking God to remove these feeling from me!

The older lawyer asked, "Are you all right sir? Are you okay to continue?"

"Yes, thank you!" then hit the play button on the remote control, the younger lawyer asked questions as the senior counsel sat and listened. All the questions were answered without hesitation, no problem. It seemed as if the younger attorney asking the question was becoming a little aggravated with me, he asked, "Was security aware of their reason for being present?"

"Yes! They had to be, the lights on the table got bright, and a few old security guards were sent to my table to observe what was going on!"

"What was their reason for being there?"

"Like I said, to observe and protect the clients' money and do security shit!"

"WHO CALLED THEM DOWN THERE?"

Putting my finger over my mouth to tell the attorney that his voice was getting a little loud I whispered, "My son is in his room, so let's keep our voice down." Looked over at the senior counsel who remained quiet, so we continued with the interview. Step by step I was able to narrate exactly what happened frame by frame in the video.

"Were you afraid at any time to do your job?"

"Absolutely not, there was no reason to be afraid or even a little intimidated, that's not my money, and I don't get paid to fight for it, that's what security is for! Should I have been?"

"OKAY, I'M ASKING THE QUESTION!" Once again, I put my hand over my lips to indicate he needed to be a little quieter. Completely satisfied with my actions that day on the casino floor, not wanting to change a thing, my adversaries were clearly cowards. Smiling while watching myself fight, never seen myself rumble and demonstrate such skills. Toward the end, the part of the video that of most interest to me was about to come on.

Already annoyed looking at the old ass guards they sent down to the table, it was clear that the guards were afraid, not to mention this fight should have never taken place! As we looked at the tape, you see me out of the right-top corner of the tape walking up to the big guy who snuck me straight to the eye. At that point, patting myself on the back and smiling, knowing how to rumble. As the fight was being broken up, the older lawyer asked me to pause the video. Then the younger lawyer asks me, "What was going on at this point, as you're walking back out in the aisle?"

"Sitting on a stool, look up at the cat-walk mirrors, seeing that my eye was swollen, then realizing he hadn't knock me out, we were just getting started. I was just going back out there to welcome him to Brooklyn."

"Brooklyn?"

"Yeah Brooklyn!"

"Okay!"

"Getting close enough to plant my feet, squared up and caught him totally off guard with a straight punch, with fire behind it, straight to his right eye. The pure power from my body buckled his knees." Replayed that part three times and each time we watched it, we all said, "Ohhh!" at the same time. This was my first time seeing the full power of that right punch of mine.

One of the lawyers asked, "Where did you learn how to

fight?" Laughing, couldn't help but think of Joe V, the Atlantic City cop who used to play boxing with me as a young kid, in front of Cramer's Supermarket in Atlantic City. He showed me how to make a fist that will take the wind out of a man, and my pops left-hand sleeper. When he caught you with that left hand, you went to sleep! Whenever used, it works perfectly. All the rumbles in Central Jr. High in Atlantic City and behind Atlantic City High school on Trenton Avenue, my skills were tested in combat. It felt good watching me rumble on video, a matter of fact we all agreed on that day in my kitchen that my rumbling skills were on point!

Then signed all the statements and documents they asked to and asked them, "Can I get a copy of this videotape?" They replied, "Yes, but not now!"

"Well, when will be a good time for me to get a copy?"

"Probably after we go to trial!"

"Okay, what about the situation I explained to your secretary about New York?"

"Oh, the glass?"

"Yeah, the glass!"

"If you go to New York, take a toothbrush with you because you're going to jail!"

"Yes, but what can you do about making some type of arrangement for me seeing a judge first?"

"Well, right now it would be a conflict of interest with the case that we already have."

"So why didn't you tell me that when we were talking

on the phone?"

"Tell you what?"

"That it could be a conflict of interest?"

"Well."

"Well? Why didn't you say that when you first spoke to me on the phone?"

"Because your case isn't a priority to me!"

"Understood but I'm not asking you to defend me, I'm asking you to call up the courts and find out what is needed to get this New York shit behind me! And how much time will I do?"

"I CAN'T DO IT AT THIS POINT AND TIME!"

It was his third time shouting at me and in my home, as the senior partner just sat there looking at him saying nothing. This all made me feel like being in the presence of Robert B. Clark all over again. Another lawyer getting what he wanted and saying fuck you to me, as if he was a bully. This young lawyer's attitude was disrespectful and shitty toward me the whole time during the damn interview. It seemed like he wanted to ignore my Trump situation but focused on his Trump shit, which was understandable but not acceptable. "Why did you tell me on the phone that you have lawyers in New York that could handle it?"

"We do!"

"But if you knew that your intention wasn't to help me, why did you come down here?"

"As I explained to you on the phone, we are representing

our client's interest."

"So, that means you don't have to keep your part of the agreement? You're not even going to look into it?"

"After the trial, I'll look into it."

"How long is that going to take?"

"Maybe six months or so!"

"That's the soonest?"

"YES!" He slammed down his folder on my table with an arrogant attitude, I put my finger up to my mouth to remind him again of the loud noise he was making but enough was enough. It was time for a reality check with this young lawyer.

"Excuse me gentlemen." Walking out of the kitchen to my bedroom, needing this lawyer to feel exactly what I felt when he said six months, the feeling of helplessness.

Walking back into the kitchen, still hearing the younger lawyer's mouth running a hundred miles an hour, until he heard that sound, that one universal sound that everyone knows. Crauk Shanke!

"OK. Let's start this conversation over." Sitting there with my old ass pump shotgun, knowing it wasn't loaded I said, "Let me introduce you to my little friend. This is Fat-ass!"

The young lawyer tried to take three steps back but had nowhere to run or go to, he was so close to the senior counsel it really looked like they were dating.

"Please, put the gun down! Please, please, please put the gun down!" he screamed.

"Now let's try this again! I have a problem in New York City. You assured me on the phone that you can investigate it. The question now is, when can you look into it?" It was the second time that day hearing the senior counsel's voice.

He said, "I can make a phone call to the courts tomorrow, but I may not hear anything until Monday!"

Setting the shotgun down, the younger lawyer still refused to look up and see that the gun was down. Instead, he said, "Put the gun down please, please, please put the gun down!"

The senior counsel was advising me on all the options he can do for me while his partner continued with such a soft voice, he began to sound like a chorus of backup singers from a Barry White song.

He continued, "Please, please, please put the gun down. Please, please, please put the gun down. Please, please, please put the gun down!" He still refused to look up at the two of us. After the senior counsel finished talking, he assured me that he would make the call personally tomorrow, but not to expect to hear anything until Monday or so. As we both look each other in the eye, we agreed on truces and shook hands. An awful smell was coming out of nowhere, it was getting stronger by the second. We both looked over at the other lawyer, who held his head down on the table, just refusing to make eye contact with either one of us. Then one more time we went over his plan.

We shook hands again and agreed on the resolution as the younger gentleman looked at both of us, grabbed his bag and walked out my back door. We both could smell something on him, I just hoped he didn't stain my booth. Walked the older lawyer to the front door, before opening it, I broke the shotgun down so he could see that there were no shells in the gun. We looked each other in the eye and shook hands again. Then he said, "Give me until next Thursday. I should have heard from the courts by then."

"Thanks, my friend."

"I may not be able to defend you right now, but if you have any questions here's my card, call me."

"Thank you."

Grabbed the doorknob then stopped, we looked at the younger lawyer getting in the car. We could see him, but he couldn't see us, the cold air was hitting his ass. "You know you're going to have a long ride home with him!"

"Yeah, I'll stop at the rest area so he can clean himself up."

"You saw his little attitude."

"Yeah, we'll have a talk on the way home about that."

"Tell him I apologize, and for him to learn to be a little nicer and kinder."

He burst out laughing uncontrollably until I had to leave the front door close for an extra minute. As he regained his composure and then walked out. The younger lawyer was the driver so he couldn't see my face as he smokes a cigarette. Just before he got in the car, we made eye contact one more time, he made sure that he rolled his eyes at me, and off they went.

Several days went by, finally a call from the lawyer in North Jersey. Curious about his findings with the New York City court, it turned out to be not good or bad. He said, "Here's what I've found out about your case! The good news is, if you're not in New York City, they won't come get you. The bad news is if they do catch you in New York, be sure to have a toothbrush with you."

Yeah, the same shit as before, still needed to raise money. For now, I'll just be the **BEST** of the **WORST** night cab drivers, Atlantic City has ever seen!"

THE END

Coming soon,

Atlantic City Rated R! After Dark

That (G) Fam Luv

Family love is priceless, embrace it, cherish it, never be afraid to encourage, correct, motivate, or just listen to a family member. Remember family is our pass, present, and future. Let them know that they must be true to themselves no matter who's watching. Always believe in themselves, there's nothing more unique than you as a human person. Just be the best you can be. Your loyalty, integrity, and feelings are yours; you must be very careful who you share them with.

This book is dedicated to my Wife, who I love more than I've ever could have imagined, my two Sons, Siblings, Cousins, Nieces, Nephews, Uncle's, Aunt's, Grandkids, Friends, and Associates. **Family Is real!**

To all the lawyers that take their practices to heart, have empathy, compassion for their clients, just being a person who is willing to listen and communicates. Finally, always use good analytical skills on their client's behalf. I take my hat off to you. **THANK YOU ALL!**

ISBN: Softcover 978-1-6678-1065

Rev. date: 6/13/2022

"Oh Yeah, I'm sorry for breaking your window, Donald."